14/02

AMERICAN TROUBLEMAKERS

Isadora Duncan: Revolutionary Dancer

AMERICAN TROUBLEMAKERS

ISADORA DUNCAN:
Revolutionary Dancer

Larry Sandomir

With an Introduction by James P. Shenton

RSVP

**RAINTREE
STECK-VAUGHN**
P U B L I S H E R S
The Steck-Vaughn Company

Austin, Texas

To Mindy, who makes all things possible, and to Chelsea, Justin, and Rachel because they are where possibilities reside. To all four, with my deepest love and affection.

CONSULTANTS

Barbara Craig
Member, Board of Directors,
    Texas Association of Teachers of Dance
Former Member, Board of Directors,
    Austin Civic Ballet
Odessa, Texas

Michael Kort
Professor of Social Science
Boston University
Boston, Massachusetts

MANAGING EDITOR
Richard G. Gallin

PROJECT MANAGER
Julie Klaus

PHOTO EDITOR
Margie Foster

A Gallin House Press Book

Library of Congress Cataloging-in-Publication Data

Sandomir, Larry.
    Isadora Duncan: Revolutionary Dancer / written by Larry Sandomir; with an introduction by James P. Shenton.
        p.   cm. — (American Troublemakers)
    "A Gallin House Press Book."— T.p. verso.
    Includes bibliographical references and index.
    ISBN 0-8114-2380-8
    1. Duncan, Isadora, 1877-1927   2. Dancers — United States — Biography.   3. Modern dance.   I.Title.   II. Series.
GV1785.D8S26   1995
792.8'028'092—dc20
    [B]
                                                                94-20568
                                                                CIP
                                                                AC

Printed and bound in the United States.
1 2 3 4 5 6 7 8 9 0 LB 99 98 97 96 95 94

CONTENTS

Maps

Isadora Duncan

INTRODUCTION

by James P. Shenton

Biography is the history of the individual lives of men and women. In all lives, there is a sequence that begins with birth, evolves into the development of character in childhood and adolescence, is followed by the emergence of maturity in adulthood, and finally, concludes with death. All lives follow this pattern, although with each emerge the differences that make each life unique. These distinctive characteristics are usually determined by the particular area in which a person has been most active. An artist draws his or her specific identity from the area of the arts in which he or she has been most active. So the writer becomes an author; the musician, a performer or composer; the politician, a senator, governor, president, or statesperson. The intellectual discipline to which one is attached identifies the scientist, historian, economist, literary critic, or political scientist, among many. Some aspects of human behavior are identified as heroic, cowardly, corrupt, or just ordinary. The task of the biographer is to explain why a particular life is worth remembering. And if the effort is successful, the reader draws from it insights into a vast range of behavior patterns. In a sense, biography provides lessons from life.

Some lives become important because of the position a person holds. Typical would be that of a U.S. President in which a biographer compares the various incumbents to determine their comparative importance. Without question, Abraham Lincoln was a profoundly significant President, much more so than Warren G. Harding whose administration was swamped by corruption. Others achieve importance because of their role in a particular area. So Emily Dickinson and Carl Sandburg are recognized as important poets and Albert Einstein as a great scientist.

Implicit in the choice of biographical subjects is the idea that each somehow affected history. Their lives explain something about the world in which they lived, even as they affect our lives and that of generations to come. But there is another consideration: Some lives are more interesting than those of others. Within each life is a great story that illuminates human behavior.

7

Then there are those people who are troublemakers, people whom we cannot ignore. They are the people who both upset and fascinate us. Their singular quality is that they are uniquely different. Troublemakers are irritating, perhaps frightening, frustrating, and disturbing, but never dull. They march to their own drummer and they are original.

To be a woman in a world dominated by men in the late 19th and early 20th centuries was not easy. To succeed obliged one to try harder. It also helped to be different. Few women understood this better than the famous American dancer Isadora Duncan. Her life was tempestuous. She embraced whatever she did with passion. Before she was a teenager, she left school to become a dancer—but one who created her own kind of dance. This meant breaking from all traditional forms of dance, including ballet. For Duncan, each dance movement drew its inspiration from nature, music, and poetry. Her first appearance in New York in 1895 launched her on a long journey that took her to Europe where she then spent most of her life. Dance in America, she believed, was stuffy and without roots in the natural movements of the human body.

Her performances in Europe and the United States were met with controversy. She often danced accompanied by music not composed for dancing. Her stage appearances were breathtaking. Barefooted and enveloped in flowing garments, she revolutionized what had been thought of as the dance. The female body escaped its traditional heavy covering, but for the prim and proper, this was shocking. Isadora Duncan's dancing was a visual assertion of female emancipation.

Duncan's personal and professional life violated all the traditional norms of feminine behavior. She opposed the institution of marriage. She had two sons and a daughter without marrying their fathers. When two of the children were killed in an accident, she refused religious services. She ran a school of dance for young girls in Germany and then in France, but did not charge tuition. She even accepted an invitation to set up a school of dance in Communist Russia. For countless women, her example of restlessly probing the limits of dance reminded them that her goal was to liberate their potential.

CHAPTER ONE

Early Childhood and Family Life

She remembered fire first, at age two or three. From an upper floor window she was thrown to the waiting arms of a policeman. Her home was burning down. Her mother, panicked, was trying to save the family, but Isadora somehow found herself comforted by strange, strong arms as tragedy was averted. Isadora Duncan's early experience symbolically represented much of what was to come. For most of her extraordinary life, Duncan was pulled out of the fire by her own sense of survival and the help of men who could not resist her.

Isadora Duncan was born in San Francisco on May 26, 1877. She often changed her birth date to suit her needs. There remains debate concerning it from others, including her brother Augustin Duncan, who set his sister's birth a day and a year later. She was born by the sea, and the rhythm of the waves inspired her idea for dance movement. All the major events of her life were to happen by the sea.

Looking back on her life, Isadora Duncan once wrote, "The sea has always drawn me to it, whereas in the mountains I have a vague feeling of discomfort and a desire to fly. They always give me the impression of being a prisoner to the earth. My life and my art were born of the sea."

Angela Isadora Duncan—she always used her middle name instead of her first—was the youngest of four children. Raymond was four years older; Augustin, five years older; and Mary Elizabeth, whom everyone called Elizabeth, seven years her elder.

Dancing came early, according to Isadora. "In my mother's womb, probably as a result of the oysters and champagne—the food of Aphrodite . . . from the moment I was born it seemed that I began to agitate my arms and legs in such a fury that my mother cried, 'You see I was quite right, the child is a maniac!' But later on, placed on a baby jumper in the centre of the table I was the amusement of the entire family and friends, dancing to any music that was played."

In addition to Isadora and her brothers and sister, Isadora's father, Joseph Charles Duncan, had four children from a previous marriage. He was a journalist, a poet, and a founder and member of San Francisco's Art Association. He was also a banking officer. Joseph Charles Duncan's involvement in the San Francisco banking industry began in 1870. Seven years later he began the Union Bank, but it never got off the ground. Soon after that, he started the Fidelity Savings Bank, but it also closed. Duncan and a son-in-law, Benjamin Le Warne, were charged with felonies related to the bank and became fugitives from the law. Both were later caught in the San Francisco area after trying to escape to Nicaragua. However, a jury trial against Duncan brought no verdict. The evidence was too confusing, and the witnesses could not give testimony that proved him guilty beyond any doubt. He was tried two more times, with the same result. A fourth jury finally acquitted him.

Joseph Charles Duncan, Isadora's father, was a journalist, poet, and banker.

Soon after Isadora's birth, her father deserted the family. Their mother was the only grown-up on whom the four children could depend to support them. Isadora was only five months old when her father went into hiding to avoid capture. He was not found for almost five months, and after his lengthy battle with the law, he and

Isadora's mother got a divorce.

Isadora Mary ("Dora") Gray Duncan, known as Dora Duncan, was a musician, but she didn't earn enough from giving piano lessons to support the family. They rented two-room apartments for short periods of time before moving on. The Duncan family had learned the need to move often to keep a step ahead of the landlord, who expected his rent money.

Yet their poverty never took away their basic good nature and ability to deal with hardship. The Duncan children's not having lots of toys and play-things actually provid-

Isadora Mary ("Dora") Gray Duncan, Isadora's mother, was a piano teacher.

ed a chance for them to create their own pleasures. Their mother would contribute to this creativity by reading them stories, telling them tales, and playing the piano for them. The Duncan children loved to dance to the music of Chopin and Mendelssohn. These activities were important in allowing their imaginations to grow.

Even before Isadora began dancing to her mother's piano playing, she had been introduced to the idea of dance in tales told by her Irish grandmother, Mary Gorman Gray, Dora's moth-er. More than 30 years before Isadora's birth, her grandmother had traveled across the Great Plains and the high mountain pass-es of the West by covered wagon. That journey had taken place in 1849, when thousands of people had traveled westward to

California. Many of them had been lured by thoughts of striking it rich in the newly discovered gold-mine areas. Others heard about the wonders of the rich farmland or the boomtown conditions in the rapidly growing city of San Francisco.

Isadora's grandmother told of her trip westward when she was only 18 and her husband, Isadora's grandfather, was 21. Their first child was born during a battle between the travelers and Native Americans. She described how they finally reached San Francisco and built their first wooden house. In that house, Isadora watched as her grandmother, remembering Ireland, danced Irish jigs and sang Irish songs. She told history through lyrics and movement. It was here that young Isadora came to understand what dance could do and how much it mattered in life.

All of the children enjoyed drama. Raymond was fascinated by the 15th-century French national hero Joan of Arc, who had led French troops against the English. She had been captured and eventually burned at the stake. Raymond, at nine years old, made her the topic of his first school speech. His excitement spilled over to Isadora, who allowed one of her dolls to be set on fire. She cried and cried as the match was about to be lit, but she didn't pull back. They wanted to make Joan of Arc's burning as real as possible. That mattered a great deal. Later in life, Isadora would claim that they had felt that this make-believe was art and that art demanded giving things up, sacrificing things for its sake.

As a young child, Isadora—growing up in a single-parent household—often asked about her father. An aunt, in reply to a question about whether Isadora had a father, said he was a devil who had destroyed her mother's life. That was the picture Isadora carried around in her mind.

It was a great surprise, therefore, when Isadora at age seven opened the door to a very handsome man in a top hat. He realized that the young girl standing in front of him was his daughter, wondered aloud if this was his "Princess Pug," his favorite nickname for her, and began to smother her with hugs, kisses, and tears. Her mother and the rest of the family would have nothing to do with him, but fearless Isadora went along with him for ice cream and cake. Although she returned filled with excitement and happiness, her family still refused to see him, and he went back to his new wife and adopted family in Los Angeles.

Isadora's mother had unusual ideas for late 19th-century America. For example, she was very unhappy about religion and decided that holiday feeling was "nonsense." When Isadora was quite young, her mother told the family the secret of Santa Claus. When, at a school Christmas party, Isadora's teacher spoke lovingly of all that Santa had brought in the way of cake and candy, Isadora replied, very seriously, "I don't believe you, there is no such thing as Santa Claus." Her embarrassed teacher told Isadora that no candy would be offered to nonbelievers. "Then I don't want your candy," she replied. The teacher was shocked by this behavior, but Isadora simply declared, "I don't believe lies."

Isadora was bored and unhappy in school. In fact, she felt her formal education was useless. Depending on the teacher Isadora had, she was considered either brilliant or stupid. It was basically only a question of how much she chose to memorize. She rarely took the time or had any real desire to understand her subjects. Schooltime usually meant clock-watching until three o'clock.

She did find learning exciting in the evenings when her mother played the music of Beethoven, Schumann, Schubert, Mozart, and Chopin on the piano. It also thrilled her when her mother read to the children from the writings of Shakespeare, Shelley, Keats, and Burns.

When Isadora was a few years older, a teacher gave an assignment to class members to write their life histories to that point, Isadora's story went partly like this: "When I was five we had a cottage on 23rd Street. Failing to pay the rent, we could not remain there but moved to 17th Street, and in a short time, as funds were low, the landlord objected, so we moved to 22nd Street, where we were not allowed to live peacefully but were moved to 10th Street."

Isadora's paper continued in this way, and when the teacher read it, she accused Isadora of lying and playing a practical joke. She was sent to the principal, who, in turn, sent for Isadora's mother. "When my poor mother read the paper she burst into tears and vowed that it was only too true. Such was our nomadic existence."

When she was grown up, Isadora Duncan still hoped that

schools would change from the days of her youth. Her memory of teachers was that they showed a total lack of understanding toward children. She remembered always that "the teacher appeared to me to be an inhuman monster who was there to torture us. And of these sufferings children will never speak."

When Isadora was in her preteens and upset about the large size of her class, she told her mother that school was of no use to her anymore. She piled her hair high on her head, as was the fashion among young women in the late 1880s, and passed for 16. She claimed that she fooled everybody.

With her in-school education at an end, her learning was gained from her mother and her own curious nature. She read constantly and participated in family discussions. Isadora was especially interested in thinkers and creative people—politicians, scientists, philosophers, artists, musicians, and writers. Her brothers and sister, too, contributed to the shaping of her mind and talents. Elizabeth said many years later that she had taught Isadora to dance. The Duncans were an imaginative family who loved performing, and each encouraged and criticized the others. The dancing that Elizabeth and Isadora taught at an early age may have had its foundations in these family critiques.

Isadora also understood, from early on, the business side of dance. She would dance for neighbors' children, and in return, she rode their bicycles. When Isadora was six years old, she "had collected half a dozen babies of the neighborhood—all of them too young to walk"—sitting before her on the floor as she taught them to wave their arms. This was the young Isadora's first "school" of dance. Eventually, it was so popular that it brought payment to the small teacher.

Her classes grew so large over the years that, by age 15, Isadora declared that her own schooling was now quite unnecessary. She had a great chance to make money, which seemed far more important. Isadora, her mother, and later, sister Elizabeth taught the society dances that were popular then, like the waltz and the polka, in the homes of many wealthy families in San Francisco and Oakland.

When Isadora and her sister expanded their dance teaching to include older students, she had her first experience of puppy love. In one of her classes was a young chemist named Vernon, and she decided she was totally in love with him. She didn't tell others about her feelings, but her heart was his. They went to balls and dances together, and Isadora's journal was filled with how she felt, "floating in his arms." Conversations outside their dancing hardly went past, "How are you?" but her love for him lasted two years. When he declared he was getting married to a young Oakland woman, Isadora's heart was broken. Many loves were to follow, but Vernon, the drugstore chemist, was her first.

The Duncan children helped earn money for the family as soon as they were old enough to do so. Their mother's earnings from giving piano lessons and knitting mittens and caps was not enough to support the family. Elizabeth lived with her grandmother for a period of time so that they might have one less mouth to feed. Augustin and Raymond took jobs whenever they were offered. As they got older, Augustin drove a cart delivering newspapers to newsboys and Raymond toiled in the railroad yards. Isadora was sometimes a door-to-door salesperson, selling her mother's knitted garments and designs. When credit was tight and needed to be loosened, it also was Isadora, the most persuasive and charming of the group, who did the bargaining.

Isadora later described what happened when there was no food to eat: "I was the volunteer who went to the butcher and through my wiles induced him to give me mutton chops without payment. I was the one sent to the baker, to entice him to continue credit. . . . This was a very good education, for from learning to wheedle ferocious butchers, I gained the technique which enabled me afterwards to face ferocious managers."

In 1893, when Isadora was 16, once again her father seemed to appear out of nowhere. Her mother agreed to see him this time, and with a newly made fortune, he gave them a beautiful home. It was complete with "dancing rooms, a tennis court, a barn and a windmill." To Isadora and her siblings it must have been like a dream. The family lived there for two years, but when this fortune, like previous ones, collapsed, Isadora and her mother, brothers, and sister were forced to move once more.

During those two years, however, Isadora got to know her father, Joseph Charles Duncan, better. She found out that he was a poet, and she learned to appreciate his creativity. The understanding Isadora gained of her father lifted a curtain of darkness from her life. All her childhood seemed to have been shadowed by the mysterious puzzle of an unknown parent about whom no one would speak. "The terrible word divorce was imprinted upon the plate of my mind. . . . I was deeply impressed by the injustice of this state of things for women, and putting it together with the story of my father and mother, I decided, then and there, that I would live to fight against marriage and for the emancipation of women and for the right of every woman to have a child or children as it pleased her, and to uphold her right and her virtue. . . . I made a vow then and there that I would never lower myself to this degrading state. This vow I always kept, even when it cost me the estrangement of my mother and the miscomprehension of the world."

She dedicated herself, therefore, to art and beauty, and to the single life.

Isadora gave much of the credit for her free spirit to her mother's lack of attention and strictness. However, she also had to deal with another side of her mother's kind of child rearing. She believed her mother at times forgot about her children, lost in her music or poetry, unaware of everything around her.

Before Isadora's father's financial problems cost them their large home, the plentiful money did allow them to open a school for dance. It also permitted her brother Augustin to open a theater in the barn on the property. These projects were very popular in the area. Eventually, the success there led to family tours of the California coast. Isadora danced; Augustin read poetry; and Elizabeth, Raymond, Augustin, and Isadora acted in a comedy. They were determined to be professional performers.

The crucial element of Isadora's childhood was her constant willingness to rebel against the lack of freedom in the society in which she lived, particularly against what limited her. This character trait was combined with a growing desire to travel in order to broaden her horizons.

Her desire for independence also led Isadora to believe that fathers who said they were working in order to leave a lot of money to their children were most likely making a mistake. She wondered if they realized that such a course took all the spirit of adventure from the lives of their children. Every dollar left to them would probably make them weaker. She believed that the longest-lasting gift a child could receive was the opportunity provided by parents to become an independent person. Children should be raised to stand on their own two feet, with the ability to make decisions and solve problems. Isadora, in fact, did not at all envy the rich children she knew. When she compared her life with theirs, hers seemed to be richer in everything that mattered, despite the problems with poverty and her parents' marriage.

Isadora's system of dance at the time seemed to express her dreams and feelings about independence. She often improvised, or made steps up as she went along, on any subject that popped into her head. During a performance of one of Isadora's first dances, inspired by Longfellow's poem *The Arrow and the Song*

Isadora Duncan in San Francisco in 1889. At an early age, she began developing her distinctive ideas about dancing.

("I shot an arrow into the air, It fell to earth, I know not where."), she was seen by a family friend from Vienna, Austria. She said Isadora reminded her of the famous Austrian ballerina, Fanny Elssler, who, earlier in the century, had been noted for her warmth, sensuality, spontaneity, and folk-based themes in her dancing. Isadora later recalled that the compliment "incited me to ambitious dreams."

Isadora went to a respected ballet teacher in San Francisco, but she wasn't happy with him. She couldn't understand why standing on her toes was beautiful. She believed it was ugly and against nature. After her third lesson, she left the class and didn't come back. Ballet has very specific steps and traditional positions. Ballerinas usually dance with a stiff, erect body, eliminating any freedom of movement. Isadora Duncan believed that all movement came from inside and should be expressed freely. She also disliked the trappings of ballet—the tutus, tights, and slippers. She wanted her feet and body unrestricted.

The discipline of ballet "disturbed my dream. I dreamed of a different dance. I did not know just what it would be, but I was feeling out towards an invisible world which I divined I might enter if I found the key."

Isadora knew her art was part of her from infancy, and she realized something important: Despite her mother's attitude, which was often too carefree as a parent, her inspiration came largely from her mother. It was due to "the heroic and adventurous spirit of my mother that it was not stifled. I believe that whatever the child is going to do in life should be begun when it is very young. I wonder how many parents realize that by the so-called education they are giving their children, they are only driving them into the commonplace, and depriving them of any chance of doing anything beautiful or original. But I suppose this must be so, or who would supply us with the thousands of shop and bank clerks, etc., who seem to be necessary for organized civilized life."

Isadora rejected the material world, preferring the creative energy made real by her mother. She thought household possessions, such as furniture, were hateful, and she never wore jewelry. She did, however, love reading and was a regular visitor at one of

Oakland's public libraries. She became friendly with the librarian there, a poet, who encouraged her to read. Isadora described her as a person who glowed with fire and passion. Much later, Isadora learned that her father had been in love with the librarian. Isadora found a joy in knowing this, and her love for reading and writing grew. She wrote editorials, news stories, short stories, a journal, and even began a novel.

While Isadora's dream led her to believe she would leave San Francisco with a large acting group, her first audition was less than successful. Isadora was told what she did was no good for a theater, that it was more fitting for a church. She was advised to go home.

Isadora was shaken but not defeated. In typically determined style, she announced Chicago as her next destination. She would go with her mother. Her sister and two brothers would stay behind in San Francisco.

Dora Gray Duncan, a fiercely independent person, was clearly not very strict with her family, and especially not so with Isadora. Generally, she didn't push her children or persuade them to give up a risky project before trying it out. She wanted them to be happy and successful. Despite her absorption in her own music and poetry, she felt that their needs, desires, triumphs, and possible failures were hers as well. Thus, in mid-1895, off to Chicago she went with Isadora.

CHAPTER TWO

Early Ventures into Dance

Chicago in 1895 was a city rebuilt from the Great Chicago Fire of 1871. But it was going through a serious economic depression and a long period of high unemployment. It turned out to be no easier to make a living there than in San Francisco. One dance audition after another resulted in nothing promising. The Duncans had arrived with a small trunk, some of Isadora's grandmother's jewelry, and $25. The average yearly wage for a factory worker in 1895 was about $440. So the $25 of a hundred years ago was equal to about what a factory worker would earn in two and a half weeks today. Without any income, soon only the trunk was

Isadora Duncan. She wore unusual dance costumes that allowed the free movement of her arms and legs.

left, and mother and daughter were homeless. The lace collar that was part of Isadora's dress was sold for $10. They managed to find a room to rent and to buy a week's worth of tomatoes.

Finally, the manager of the Masonic Temple Roof Garden agreed to give Isadora work, on the condition that she spice up her dances. "You're very pretty," he said, "and graceful. And if you would change all that and do something with some pep in it, I'd engage [hire] you."

He wanted her to wear frilly dresses, and once again, Isadora's skills of persuasion were called into play. She used them on the manager of a department store, who agreed to let her take a frilly skirt on credit, with her promise to pay from her first earnings. Isadora did repay him from the $50 she made from her first week's work. But after three weeks' work, she refused to sign a long-term contract at the Masonic Temple Roof Garden. She found such cabaret-style dancing horrible, and she "had enough of trying to amuse the public with something which was against my ideals. And that was the first and last time I ever did so."

As the summer of 1895 was drawing to a close, money was again in short supply. Isadora discovered that theatrical producer Augustin Daly and his theater company, starring Ada Rehan, were in Chicago. Daly had a reputation as the most art-loving theater manager in the United States. He loved beauty. Not only had he written several popular plays, he also produced Shakespeare's comedies and adaptations of successful French and German plays. Isadora asked for but was refused a meeting with him for some time. However, she was determined and kept trying to see him. Finally one evening her persistence was rewarded.

In her usual breathless, emotional style, Isadora presented her case:

> I have a great idea to put before you, Mr. Daly, and you are probably the only man in this country who can understand it. I have discovered the dance. I have discovered the art which has been lost for two thousand years. You are a supreme theatre artist, but there is one thing lacking in your theatre which made the old Greek theatre great, and this is the art of the

dance—the tragic chorus. Without this it is a head and body without legs to carry it on. I bring you the dance. I bring you the idea that is going to revolutionize our entire epoch. Where have I discovered it? By the Pacific Ocean, by the waving pine-forests of Sierra Nevada. I have seen the ideal figures of youthful America dancing over the top of the Rockies.

The supreme poet of our country is Walt Whitman. I have discovered the dance that is worthy of the poems of Walt Whitman. I am indeed the spiritual daughter of Walt Whitman. For the children of America I will create a new dance that will express America. I will bring to your theatre the vital soul that it lacks, the soul of the dancer.

For you know that the birth of the theatre was the dance, that the first actor was the dancer. He danced and sang. That was the birth of the tragedy, and until the dancer in all his spontaneous great art returns to your theatre, your theatre will not live in its true expression!

After his shock wore off a bit, an exhausted Augustin Daly could only reply, "Well, I have a little part in a pantomime that I am putting on in New York. You can report for rehearsals the first of October and if you suit you are engaged. What's your name?"

"My name is Isadora," she replied.

"Isadora. That's a pretty name," he said. "Well, Isadora, I'll see you in New York on the first of October."

With that, Isadora was filled with the excitement that only being appreciated can bring. She made plans for a New York autumn.

New York City had the great art Isadora expected, and it had one more thing: the sea. With the inspiration of the sea in her heart, she went to the Broadway theater known officially as Daly's Theater where she was informed there was a part for her in the pantomime show—no speaking allowed—starring the famous French comedian Jane May. Isadora took the role, happy to be accepted but disappointed because pantomime was not part of her dream. To her, pantomime was neither acting nor dance.

Rehearsals brought reality to her fears. Jane May, despite her small size, was an explosive personality. She was very hard on Isadora and let Augustin Daly know clearly that here was a person of no talent, a person who was unable to handle the role. With the thought of a return to poverty in her mind, tears ran down Isadora's cheeks. Daly viewed this scene and replied to Jane May, "You see, she is very expressive when she cries. She'll learn."

Time passed and rehearsals became more involved. Movements that had at first seemed horrifying to Isadora now caused her to admire "the extraordinary and vibrant expression of the pantomime actress." Yet the silence and gestures of pantomime continued to frustrate her, although the $15 a week she received once the show opened helped the family survive. After two months on the road, the troupe returned to New York City, having failed financially. Jane May went back to Paris, and Daly offered Isadora a part in the fairy scene of Shakespeare's *A Midsummer Night's Dream*. Isadora accepted the job but felt the role was another blow to her dreams. She wished to express the feelings and emotions of humanity; the role she had been offered certainly didn't provide a good opportunity for that.

Her costume consisted of a long straight tunic, a flowing shirt of white and gold gauze, and two sparkling wings. Isadora felt the wings were unnecessary. She believed she could—by means of dance movements—"show" the wings without putting on costume ones. Even a surprise performance prior to opening night, where she danced alone in front of an applauding public, failed to move Augustin Daly to give her greater artistic freedom. In fact, Daly punished Isadora's expression of individuality by darkening the lights whenever she performed.

She stayed with Daly's group for a year and saw her salary increase to $25 a week, but Isadora remained deeply unhappy. Her dreams, hopes, and desires all appeared impossible to achieve.

The Duncan family, which had come together in New York City, stayed in a studio with five mattresses on the floor. Isadora wanted the place free of furniture to allow for dance space. Expenses were met by renting out the studio to teachers of various arts. For several months in 1897, Isadora traveled in England with Daly's theatrical troupe and performed in London and at Stratford-upon-Avon.

In 1898, Duncan decided to end her business relationship with Augustin Daly, who she felt had misused her talents. "What's the good of having me here, with my genius," she asked him, "when you make no use of me?"

Duncan in *A Midsummer Night's Dream*.

It was then that Isadora Duncan was drawn to the music of Ethelbert Woodbridge Nevin, an American composer of songs and piano pieces. She created dances to some of his works, such as "Narcissus," "Ophelia," and "Water Nymphs." One day, she was practicing her dances, when without warning, Nevin who was working in a nearby studio, burst in.

"I hear you are dancing to my music! I forbid it, I forbid it! It isn't dance music, my music. Nobody shall dance it."

After his tantrum, Duncan sat him down, asked him to watch her, and promised that if he didn't like what he saw, she'd never do the dances again.

She danced to "Narcissus." In ancient Greek mythology, Narcissus was the handsome son of a river god and a water nymph. Although warned never to look upon his own features, Narcissus fell in love with his own reflection, which he had never seen before, in the waters of a spring. But since the reflection in the water could not return his love, Narcissus died of despair and was turned into a flower that bears his name, the narcissus. Isadora Duncan moved inside the character of Narcissus to create such movement and beauty that, upon her finishing her dancing, Nevin jumped up and declared, "You are an angel. You are a *divinatrice* [fortune-teller]. Those very movements I saw when I was composing the music."

Nevin became so carried away with the beauty of Duncan's dance that, on the spot, he created an original piece for her. He called it "Spring." He proposed that the two should do some concerts together at Carnegie Hall's music room, called the Lyceum. He would accompany her on the piano.

These Nevin-Duncan concerts were so successful that, if they had thought ahead and hired a manager, their careers would have been made. Yet, as Isadora later remembered, they were surprisingly innocent about such business matters. The Carnegie performances began on March 24, 1898, and they did lead to engagements in many New York society homes. Isadora even danced to Edward FitzGerald's version of the *Rubaiyat*, the famous Persian poem of Omar Khayyám, which was sometimes read aloud by her brother Augustin or her sister Elizabeth.

With that summer came an invitation to dance at Newport,

Rhode Island, in Mrs. Astor's villa. In the 1880s and 1890s, Newport had become a summer resort where American millionaires built huge summer mansions, some with hundreds of rooms and larger than many European palaces. So when Mrs. Astor, wife of a multimillionaire invited Isadora Duncan to perform, it was as if royalty had commanded her, for "Mrs. Astor represented to America what a Queen did to England. The people who came into her presence were more awed and frightened than if they had approached royalty."

Mrs. Astor and Isadora Duncan got along well, though, and dances were held in other Newport mansions. Yet the pay was very low, and Isadora and her family hardly had enough to get by. More important to Isadora, however, was what finally led to her disappointment. It was her knowledge that these high-society women "hadn't any of them the slightest understanding of what I was doing. . . . [T]hese people seemed so enwrapped in snobbishness and the glory of being rich that they had no art sense whatever." Duncan was even more upset to see that these women "considered artists as inferior—a sort of upper servant."

For Isadora Duncan, New York was losing its luster, and Isadora dreamed of London, where she believed there was magic in art and writing. She also felt that for all the experience gained in New York, she found no real understanding or support for her ideas about letting the body express what dancing was. She had an attitude about dance and the human body being united that had not yet been really understood and appreciated.

The biggest gap between her and the public, she believed, was in her total opposition to ballet, which was at that time the only area really open to a serious dancer. She saw ballet as a false art because it was unnatural. It contained too many required moves, holds, starts, and stops. There was, in Isadora's eyes, no flow. The toe-dancing aspect even worked against the structure of the human body.

This lack of sympathy and understanding from her potential audience left her without a real direction. When she tried to reach a larger audience, she was ignored. She was even criticized for being too much like a lady, too classic, and for avoiding the popular dances of Broadway. She certainly did not add many fans from the wealthy levels of society when she danced in a costume that showed bare arms and legs. To these patrons, such a revealing outfit was shocking.

Another episode pushed young Isadora further away from the idea of remaining in New York. She, her mother, and her sister had leased two rooms on the first floor of the Windsor Hotel on stylish Fifth Avenue and Forty-seventh Street. They hoped this

An 1898 photograph of Isadora Duncan taken in New York City. She is wearing her mother's lace curtains.

fancy address might attract and impress rich patrons whose children would come to them for dancing lessons. It was St. Patrick's Day, 1899. Isadora and Elizabeth were teaching a class of 30 children, and their mother, Dora Duncan, was playing the piano. They could hear the parade marchers and bands outside the window, which they found annoying. But something strange began to attract their attention. Dora Duncan looked up from her piano to see a woman's body fly past the window. She believed she was imagining things, but it happened again. They went to the door, only to find the hallway filled with smoke. The building was on fire. People were jumping from the higher floors. Calmly, the Duncan women helped gather up the children and got them to safety before the collapse of most of the building.

The family then moved to Fifth Avenue's Hotel Buckingham, but Isadora was still in shock. She told newspaper reporters that all she was able to save was the dress she wore, "a house gown of dark brown material with flaring Elizabethan collar." It was striking that she brought that up, because, even in poverty, in shock, and eventually when she became world famous, flaring and flowing collars and shawls always seemed to be part of Isadora Duncan's wardrobe.

The family of four children and their mother no longer lived together, for Augustin Duncan had fallen in love during a road company production of Shakespeare's *Romeo and Juliet*. His wife was only 16 when he announced to his family that he was married. Dora Duncan's reaction was similar to her reaction when her ex-husband had come back the first time. She exploded, turned on her heel, went to another room, and slammed the door. Augustin was terribly upset, and it was left for Isadora to show family sympathy. She went with her brother to see his wife. They climbed the five flights of stairs to the walk-up apartment where Romeo's Juliet lay. She was a pretty young woman, but quite weak and sick. Husband and wife were expecting a baby.

Duncan was still in New York, with dreams of a great future across the Atlantic, when the spring of 1899 began with no money or job prospects. Her creative mind went into action. She decided to ask those women who had previously hired her to dance in their homes for enough money to get her family to London.

One rich woman, whose home overlooked Manhattan's Central Park at Fifty-ninth Street, seemed taken with Isadora's story, went right to her checkbook, and handed over a check for $50, nowhere near enough to make London a reality. At her second stop, this time on Fifth Avenue, Duncan was received coldly. She was refused at first any help at all. Clearly, a serious problem was that her skill was not in ballet. It took a fainting spell by Isadora, for she hadn't eaten all day, before another $50 was offered. The condition was that it be returned when Isadora made money. She never did repay it; when she had earned large amounts of money, the poor received it instead.

Several more such efforts gave her an additional $200, which did not leave the Duncans enough to purchase second-class tickets on a steamship. They would certainly not have anything left over once Isadora, Elizabeth, Raymond, and their mother reached London. But Raymond pleaded their case with the captain of a cattle boat, who was so touched, he took them on as passengers.

Before leaving New York, the family performed a farewell concert, which met with sarcasm and controversy in a report from a local paper. Duncan's costume was described as "a surgical bandage of gauze and satin of the hue of raspberry ice, with streamers of various lengths." The audience was described as "tortured souls [who] gazed at one another and blushed or giggled according to their individual form of nervousness." The ending of the show brought relief that Isadora Duncan's costume had not fallen off. The writer sarcastically wondered at Duncan's decision to go to England because peaceful relations between the United States and England might change negatively upon her arrival.

For the journey, an embarrassed Isadora Duncan became Maggie O'Gorman, and the family referred to themselves as the O'Gorman family.

CHAPTER 3

Discovery of a Dream—England

The two-week trip in 1899 landed the "O'Gorman" clan in the seaport of Hull, England, in May. The family group took the train to London and reclaimed the Duncan name a few hours later. They found a place to stay through a newspaper ad and spent much of their first few days in London sight-seeing. Only the rent bill brought the family back to earth. They returned from a lecture at the National Gallery, which has a superb collection of paintings, statues, and sculptures, to find their baggage on the street and the door locked. With only six shillings left to their name, the Duncans were left to wonder what would happen to them next.

Isadora Duncan saw their plight, a bit exaggerated, as out of a Charles Dickens novel, where poverty was always part of the plot. She was shocked "that we youngsters could remain cheerful through such a series of disasters." Yet even more astonishing was "that my poor mother, who had already experienced so many hardships and troubles in her life, and who was no longer young, could take them as the ordinary run of things."

Without payment in advance, no hotel would take them in unless they put their luggage up as a deposit. Lodging houses turned them away as well. The end of the day found them on a bench in London's Green Park, and even from there, a policeman had them move on.

Their lives went on like this for four days, until Isadora had had enough. She took her mother, Raymond, and Elizabeth and marched into one of the city's finest hotels. "I informed the night porter, who was half asleep, that we had just come on the night train, that our luggage would come on from Liverpool, to give us rooms in the meantime, and to order breakfast to be sent up to us, consisting of coffee, buckwheat cakes and other American delicacies."

Their plan worked for yet another day. When they felt they had gone as far as they could go with it, they simply walked out of the hotel, "but this time without waking the night porter!"

Revived and ready again, the Duncans were working their way through the Chelsea area of London. Isadora Duncan spied a paragraph in a newspaper saying that "a certain lady, in whose house I had danced in New York, had taken a house in Grosvenor Square and was entertaining largely."

Duncan went to see her and was greeted warmly. She told the woman that she was in London dancing in drawing rooms.

"That would be just the thing for my dinner party on Friday night," the woman said. "Could you give some of your interpretations after dinner?"

With great hope of exposure to a wider audience, and a small advance—that is, a prepayment of some of the money—in her hands, Duncan sped back to Chelsea and her family. The money enabled them to rent a studio and buy some food.

Isadora Duncan bought a few yards of veiling for her performance and danced three numbers to her mother's accompaniment. Despite overheard whispers in the audience about why she looked so very sad, all went well and her employer was pleased.

Interestingly, no one in the quiet audience commented on Isadora Duncan's costume, which was different from anything they had seen before. The costume was inspired by the clothing of the ancient Greeks. She had been inspired by a visit to the British Museum where the Elgin Marbles, the beautiful marble sculptures from Athens's ancient Parthenon, were on display. Isadora Duncan danced wearing transparent veils and sandals, with her legs and feet stockingless—certainly unusual during an era when a woman exposing her ankles was regarded as shocking. The originality of her dance, moreover, brought disappointing comments, such as "How pretty" and "Thank you very much."

Duncan was in no position to complain, however, because many invitations to dance in the homes of the wealthy followed this first outing. Some offered her pay, some did not, but being seen dancing was always part of the plan. Duncan realized this, and neither she nor her mother ever complained. Rather, they ate

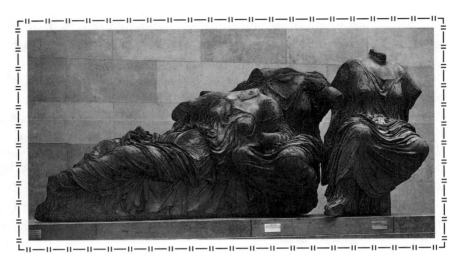

Ancient Greek marble sculptures, such as *Three Goddesses* on display at the British Museum, inspired Isadora Duncan's costume.

less in order to be able to spend what they had on proper clothing and appearance.

As September approached, Elizabeth made the decision to go back to the United States to make money. She believed if she did that, she could send some to Isadora. Since she assumed that her sister would soon be rich and famous, Elizabeth believed that she would be able to return to Isadora soon.

The departure left the remaining Duncans very lonely. Isadora, Raymond, and their mother often spent the long October days shut away in their studio "wrapped in blankets, playing chequers on an impoverished chequer-board with pieces of cardboard." Things got so bad that they slept in all day, unable to face their serious financial problems.

Finally, some money came from Elizabeth who was doing well teaching dance in New York. Their outlook was now at least a little brighter, and with hope came opportunity.

Isadora and Raymond were dancing in the gardens of one of the parks one early autumn evening when a beautiful woman happened by. "Where on earth did you people come from?"

"Not from the earth at all," replied Isadora, "but from the moon."

"Well," she said, "whether from the earth or the moon, you are very sweet; won't you come and see me?"

The beautiful woman turned out to be Mrs. Patrick Campbell, one of England's most famous actresses. When they visited her, Mrs. Patrick Campbell played the piano, sang, and recited poetry for the Duncans. In return, Isadora Duncan danced for her. Mrs. Patrick Campbell was so taken with the young woman's talent that she introduced her to Mrs. George Wyndham, whose husband was a scholar and a member of Parliament, the British law-making body. He had recently edited a version of Plutarch's *Lives* of the ancient Greeks and Romans and also an edition of Shakespeare's poems. Mrs. George Wyndham arranged a performance for Isadora Duncan in her home. Many of London's great artists and literary people were there. At this gathering, Isadora Duncan met the artist Charles Hallé, nearly 50, and son of a famous pianist. Isadora Duncan was attracted to no one else, though many younger men were interested in her. This middle-aged man, despite being round-shouldered, was an attractive figure, at least for Duncan. His gray hair was parted in the middle and fell over his ears. Most pleasing to Duncan, though, was his special, sweet expression. Charles Hallé held Duncan's attention like no other.

Hallé was director of the New Gallery, where modern painters showed their work. He felt that Isadora Duncan should dance there, and so she gave three performances at the New Gallery, one in March 1900 and two in July. The third program, her best received, was inspired by Renaissance paintings: Botticelli's *La Primavera; Angel with a Violin*, whose idea came from a painting by Cesare Negri; and Titian's *Bacchus and Ariadne*. She danced in the main area, around a fountain that was surrounded by exotic plants, flowers, and palms. The first and second recitals were introduced by speeches by Andrew Lang, a noted Scottish expert on folklore, mythology, and ancient Greece, and by Sir Charles Hubert Purry, a famous English composer and musical historian. Several of her dances were based on ancient Greek poetry, which was read by a scholar on ancient Greece while she performed. Duncan also danced to music by Mendelssohn and to "Water Nymphs" by Nevin, the contemporary American composer, and in her second recital to music by Chopin and Gluck. The audience of artists and intellectuals was thrilled. Newspaper reviews were enthusiastic, and Hallé was overwhelmed with Duncan's success. She was even introduced to the Prince of Wales, who declared her a "Gainsborough beauty."

Some of the other reviews of this new talent spoke of a special grace, eloquent gestures, and artistic pleasure. Descriptions mentioned visions of flowers and birds, her beautiful stage presence, and the flowing arm and hand movements.

This success allowed the family to move to a large studio and gave Duncan new inspiration. Her happiness was increased when Douglas Ainslie, a poet from Oxford, came into her life.

Duncan was attracted to Ainslie's tender voice and thoughtful eyes. He loved reading aloud, and she loved listening to him each night after he came in, at twilight, with volumes of verse under his arms. Even though Isadora's mother would be there as a chaperone, boredom would overcome Dora Duncan each time, and she would fall asleep. It was then that Douglas would lean over and kiss the young woman on the cheek.

So happy was Isadora Duncan, that beyond Douglas Ainslie and Charles Hallé, she had no need for any other friends. She was unaffected by the other men who were interested in her and turned them away with an attitude that she

Duncan, inspired by Botticelli's painting *La Primavera*, dances with her feet bare.

later described as "so superior that they were completely frozen."

Unfrozen, however, was intellectual and artistic society's view of Isadora Duncan's talent. Upon dancing Mendelssohn's "Spring Song" for the actress Lady Tree, she was praised at a banquet as one of the world's greatest artists. "I have awakened a frenzy of enthusiasm in such men as Andrew Lang, Watts [a painter], Sir Edwin Arnold [a poet and journalist], Austin Dobson [a poet and biographer], Charles Halle—in all the painters and poets whom I had met in London." Yet respect from general audiences still eluded her. Theater managers remained less than thrilled with her performances. Nevertheless, with the companionship of Ainslie and Hallé, winter passed happily for Isadora Duncan. But for Raymond Duncan, there was boredom. He left London for Paris, and soon after, in midsummer 1900, his mother and Isadora followed. Once in France, the Duncan women took the train, and Raymond met them, with his unusually long hair flowing over his ears.

After renting a studio, brother and sister spent a great amount of time in the Louvre. They especially studied the museum's collection of ancient Greek statues and vases. They returned there every day and had to be almost forcibly removed at closing time. Even with no friends and no money, they were happy. The Louvre had enough to satisfy their appetites endlessly.

Time passed in this summertime paradise. One morning, seemingly out of nowhere, Charles Hallé appeared. He became Isadora's daily guide, over Raymond's objections. She and Charles wandered through historic buildings and museums, dined at the Eiffel Tower, went to the country on Sundays, and journeyed through the gardens of Versailles and the forest of Saint-Germain. Duncan danced for Charles Hallé in the forest, and he made drawings of her. They visited the Universal Exposition of 1900. There Duncan was especially entranced by the sculptures of the great French sculptor Auguste Rodin. Perhaps she was attracted to the way he had treated the human form in movement and to the force of his sculpture. Summer in Paris continued to be a paradise for Isadora Duncan, although it was somewhat less so for her mother and brother, who felt left out.

Charles Hallé returned to London once autumn came and

Duncan studied movement as depicted in ancient Greek sculpture.

asked his nephew, Charles Noufflard, to watch over Duncan. Noufflard visited her frequently. He also introduced her to a young man, Jacques Beaugnier, who requested his mother, Madame de St. Marceau, a sculptor's wife, to have Isadora Duncan dance for her friends.

"I danced before a group of people so kind, so enthusiastic, that I was quite overcome. They scarcely waited for the end of a dance to call out, 'Bravo, bravo, comme elle est exquise! Quel enfant!'"

They spoke of how wonderful it was that such beauty could come from one so young.

Isadora Duncan soon threw herself into her study of dance movement, in search of what would be "the divine expression of the human spirit through the medium of the body's movement." After long periods of deep thought, she finally found the center of her passion. Duncan described it as "the crater of motor power, the unity from which all diversities of movements are born, the mirror of vision for the creation of the dance." From this moment of light, the theory on which her school was founded, came to be.

While ballet had movement that resulted in something unnatural, in Isadora Duncan's view, like a well-handled marionette, her vision "sought the source of the spiritual expression to flow into the channels of the body filling it with vibrating light—the centrifugal force reflecting the spirit's vision." This feeling of everything coming together, she felt, could be communicated through dance.

What seemed difficult to explain to grown-ups was easily understood even by the youngest children. They were able to listen to their hearts and experience the awakening that is the start of the journey of dance. This journey, Duncan believed, filled all movements, even separate from actual dance. She felt that children create a physical grace that is a real part of who they are. Dance becomes their nature. Isadora Duncan had founded a new philosophy of human movement, and she implemented her beliefs when dancing to the works of such masters as Chopin and Gluck. Her mother was almost always her accompanist and never minded repeating the entire score of Gluck's *Orpheus and Euridice* all night until morning dew appeared on the grass.

The premier society matron in 1901 was Countess Greffuhle, who invited Duncan to perform before many Parisian celebrities in her drawing room. The countess praised her as a "renaissance of Greek Art." Another important experience for her was at the studio of Madame Madeleine Lemaire, where she danced to the music of Gluck's *Orpheus and Euridice.*

In addition to her actual performing, Isadora Duncan researched dance history in great detail at the Library of the Opera. She was determined to read everything that had ever been written on the art of dancing. She began with the earliest Egyptians and moved to the present day. She made lengthy notes of everything she read.

Isadora Duncan's involvement in her new ideas of dance and the effects of her connection with Countess Greffuhle bore fruit. One afternoon, she met another high-society person, the Princess de Polignac. The princess told Duncan that when she saw her dance, Duncan's art interested her and her composer husband.

Despite what Duncan at first regarded as the princess's "imposing stature," "cold looks and the tone of her voice," Duncan soon concluded that the princess by her demeanor was simply hiding shyness and a sensitive nature. So Duncan went on to discuss her art and dreams with her. The princess "at once offered to arrange a concert . . . in her studio. . . . The Princess seemed to sense the poverty of our bare, cold studio and our pinched look, for, when abruptly leaving, she shyly placed an envelope on the table, in which we found two thousand francs."

She got along beautifully with the princess and the prince,

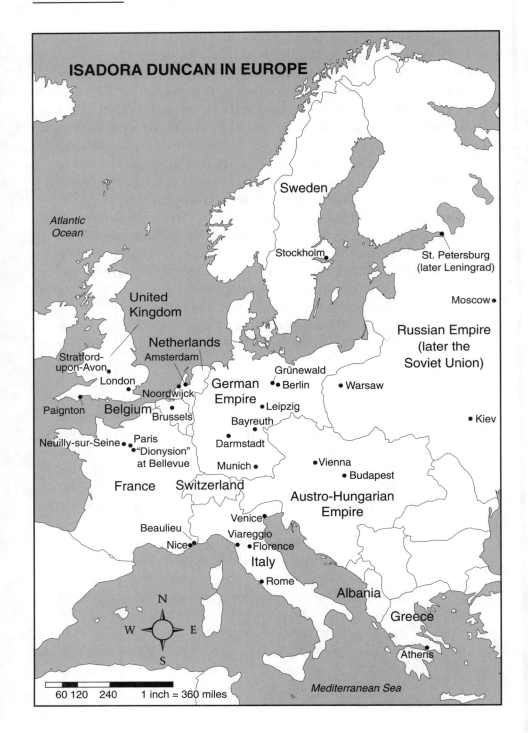

ISADORA DUNCAN IN EUROPE

Atlantic Ocean

Sweden

Stockholm

St. Petersburg (later Leningrad)

Moscow

United Kingdom

Russian Empire (later the Soviet Union)

Netherlands

Amsterdam

Grünewald
Berlin

Warsaw

Stratford-upon-Avon

German Empire

London

Noordwijck

Leipzig

Paignton

Belgium

Bayreuth

Kiev

Brussels

Darmstadt

Neuilly-sur-Seine

Paris
"Dionysion" at Bellevue

Munich

Vienna

Budapest

France

Switzerland

Austro-Hungarian Empire

Beaulieu

Venice

Nice

Viareggio
Florence

Italy

Rome

Albania

Greece

Athens

N
W   E
S

60 120   240   1 inch = 360 miles

Mediterranean Sea

who was "a fine musician of considerable talent; an exquisite, slight gentleman, who always wore a little black velvet cap, which framed his delicate, beautiful face." He saw Isadora Duncan as his long-awaited vision and dream. They seemed to understand each other and were ready to work together.

The performance was a great success, and a series of concerts sponsored by the noble couple was arranged. A frequent attendee at these 1901 performances was the noted French painter and lithographer Eugène Carrière. He declared that the dance of Isadora Duncan was no longer just amusement. It was something from deep within, as a work of art more alive than any known before. It was a way of pushing the audience to feel emotions and appreciate dance at levels they were meant to reach.

Besides Carrière, Duncan met another friend for life in Mary Desti. Although divorced (unusual for that period) and with an infant son, Desti had left Chicago and traveled to Paris, where she said she had come to study singing. Mary devoted herself completely to her Isadora. Her open, disordered, spontaneous way of behaving gave Duncan permission to be carefree—something she missed at times while growing up in the United States.

Curiously, with this inner freedom blooming, Isadora Duncan looked into dance technique far more closely. She favored exercises designed to create smoothness of movement, like walking, running, skipping, and leaping. She avoided anything in her dance movements that created stops and starts too often. Most of what she wanted to express was developed in constant rehearsing. Her dance movements seemed simple to an audience because they were so fluid. Nevertheless, her methods would prove to be challenging for even the best pupils of dance to master. Yet, once the key movements were understood, the dance had a grace unknown before. That grace was able to vividly express deep feelings, such as fear or love. The art was personal, based on what a dancer brought to the performance in addition to her or his technical ability. This is the way modern dance, as we know it today, is approached. Universal feelings are expressed for all to appreciate.

"I am not a dancer," Duncan once stated. "I am here to make you listen to the music." She went within the music in an effort to use dance to make the music more meaningful. Perfecting this technique became the most important aspect of her life. By this approach, she felt she could involve herself in the meaning of the music and then express it to the audience. The notion of dancing to music not originally created for dance was unheard of and very controversial. Her dance was infused with music's emotion, and she gave it creative physical expression.

Duncan's sense of fate and purpose allowed her—although she had little money—to turn away anyone who could not fully appreciate what she did. She even rejected a Berlin producer, Alexander Grosz, who offered her a high beginning salary to perform at the city's largest music hall.

"We have heard of your barefoot art . . . there will be much money. I already offer you five hundred marks a night. There will be more later. You will be magnificently presented as the 'First Barefoot Dancer in the World.'"

"Certainly not. Certainly not," declared Isadora Duncan. "Not on any terms."

"But this is impossible. I cannot take no for an answer. I have the contract ready."

"No," she explained. "My Art is not for a music hall. I will come to Berlin some day, and I hope to dance to your Philharmonic Orchestra, but in a Temple of Music, not in a music hall with acrobats and trained animals. . . ."

Offers up to one thousand marks a night came by the next day, and these too were dismissed quickly. "I would refuse ten thousand, one hundred thousand. I am seeking something which you don't understand."

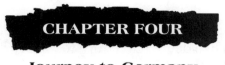

CHAPTER FOUR

Journey to Germany

Loie Fuller, an American dancer considered at that time to be a great artist, seemed to see Isadora Duncan's art more clearly than most. Fuller went to Duncan's studio, where she sat entranced, watching this amazingly talented artist dance and even discussing Duncan's revolutionary theories. Fuller suggested that Duncan join her in Berlin, Germany, in early 1902.

Once there, Duncan watched Fuller perform. "Before our very eyes she turned to many colored, shining orchids, to a wavering, flowing sea flower, and at length to a spiral-like lily, all the magic of Merlin, the sorcery of light, colour, flowing form. What an extraordinary genius!"

The more Duncan saw her dance, the more fascinated she became with Loie Fuller's unique talent. To Duncan, she was light itself. She became every color of the rainbow. It took her to another level of understanding about dance. Duncan continued to watch, and she admired the range and combination of simple dance movements and the way Fuller used light and shadow. Fuller held sticks in her hands to creatively express a flower blooming or wings fluttering. Isadora Duncan learned a great deal from Fuller's use of light to emphasize or enhance gestures. She applied much of that knowledge later in her own work.

However, despite her great respect for Loie Fuller, Fuller's traveling group was stranger than Isadora Duncan was ready to deal with. Finally, in Vienna, the Austrian capital, Duncan's roommate, named Nursey, declared that God had told her to kill Isadora. After hearing those words, Duncan asked if she could say her prayers first. Her "last wish" granted, Duncan slipped out of bed and ran out of the room with Nursey right behind. Duncan fled to where six hotel clerks managed to restrain her attacker until doctors could arrive. Once calmed down, Duncan took some time off and returned to Paris to be with her mother whom she had sorely missed during the dance tour. While in Paris, Isadora Duncan decided not to return to Fuller's dance company.

Soon after this experience, she went to Italy, where the paintings of Botticelli aroused her artistic passion and imagination. In Florence, she visited the Uffizi art museum, where she saw the *Primavera* ("The Allegory of Spring"), one of Botticelli's most famous paintings. Duncan had previously seen only copies of this beautiful work. As early as 1900, she had been inspired to create a dance that might communicate the emotions she felt emanating from it.

"I sat there until I actually saw the flowers growing, the naked feet dancing, the bodies swaying; until the messenger of joy came to me and I thought: 'I will dance this picture and give to others this message of love, spring, procreation of life which had been given to me with such anguish. I will give to them, through the dance, such ecstasy.'" Duncan felt the soul of the painting enter her body. This inspired kind of dancing became her "Dance of the Future," which she later described in a publication of the same name.

Isadora Duncan arrived in Budapest, Hungary, in April 1902. Here she signed her first contract to dance in a theater before the public. She hesitated because she felt her dancing, although highly praised by intellectuals and artists, might not be appreciated by the general public. Yet, she had finally been persuaded by manager Alexander Grosz to dance for them. From the night of her first appearance to her thirtieth, she was a huge success, dancing before sold-out houses. Duncan arranged shorter, lighter dances that were filled with a special grace. The crowning achievement was her creation for Johann Strauss's *On the Beautiful Blue Danube* waltz. It was supposedly choreographed on the spur of the moment and became one of the dances she was always known for. A review from the *Theater Magazine*, written by Gertrude Norman, read in part: "With a leap of joy like one arisen from some hiding place in the rocks and shaking off the salt fresh spray, she sways and sways 'til the big audience seems scarcely able to restrain itself." Duncan's personality was fully captured in this dance; her communication with the audience was total.

About this time, Isadora Duncan met the Hungarian actor Oscar Beregi, whom she always referred to as "Romeo." She fell in love. She was 24 years old and felt successful, worthy, and lucky. At the same time as her heart was almost bursting with love, her professional reviews raved about her. Dance and music critics wrote about her fresh approach, how much like an angel she looked, and what joy she expressed—and about her curious modesty that seemed to shine even though she allowed her bare arms and feet to be seen. They praised the brand-new movements she created, movements that went beyond what audiences had ever expected legs and feet to do. She was compared to visions of a dream that touched their souls.

The romance with Beregi, however, came to an end when she realized her role as his future wife was to be nothing more than an adornment. He felt that he would not need more from her than to simply watch his performances. He began to pay her little attention and spent much time rehearsing for the part of Brutus in Shakespeare's *Julius Caesar*. Finally, he suggested they break up. When it came down to a choice between art and love, he realized that art had won. Duncan remembered, "My last vision of him was mad enthusiasm of the theatre audience, while I sat in a box [a theater's enclosed group of balcony seats] swallowing my tears and feeling as if I had eaten bushels of broken glass."

She went off to Vienna to deal with her sadness. Before leaving, she signed a contract with Grosz to perform there and in Germany. She fell ill, however, and had to go into a hospital. Beregi heard of her illness and came to see her, but Duncan knew their love was really over.

Isadora Duncan had never paid close attention to money matters, and the family again, in 1902, found themselves in need. They telegraphed Alexander Grosz for funds to return to Berlin, where he was preparing for Duncan's debut at the Kroll Opera House early in 1903. Grosz spared no expense in the preparations for Duncan's appearance. He believed without the shadow of a doubt that Duncan would have a great triumph. His faith was amply rewarded. At her debut, which lasted more than two hours, several encores were demanded, and when they were done, the audience rushed onto the stage. Duncan was actually

43

in serious danger of being trampled by the fans. These were the same people she once worried would not be able to understand or appreciate her art.

A few months after her debut, she offered the German press an interview, where she surprised them by making a speech on the art of the dance. She stated, "The dance of the future will be one whose body and soul have grown so harmoniously together that the natural language of that soul will have become the movement of the body." The members of the press surprised Duncan, for they listened with rapt attention. They later wrote lengthy articles that treated her ideas with the respect she thought they deserved.

In May 1903, Duncan traveled to Paris for a series of performances at the Sarah Bernhardt Theater. She made sure the theater was filled on opening night by giving out free tickets, but Paris critics were cool in their praise. However, audiences warmed to her over the course of the engagement, and by July, she was declared a great artistic success.

Before the end of these performances, Duncan was invited to a picnic given in honor of Auguste Rodin's having been awarded the French Legion of Honor. At the lunch for the famous sculptor, whose sculptures of the human body Duncan had so admired, she was asked to dance. But Duncan said she couldn't because her dress was too long. She was persuaded to take it off, and she danced with such grace that Rodin was entranced. He loved her spontaneity and her freedom of movement and spirit.

Isadora and Dora Duncan with a German sculptor and his sculpture of the dancer.

CHAPTER FIVE

The Legend Grows—Greece and Austria

To further develop in the ways of inner beauty, Isadora Duncan and her family returned to a project that had always been a dream for them. They were going to Athens, Greece, a place they considered holy.

Already, before they even left, Isadora Duncan's brother Raymond had begun wearing his hair flowing over his ears and had started dressing in the ancient Greek and Roman style, wrapped in a toga and wearing sandals. His diet consisted of yogurt, goat cheese, fruit, and milk. Later, he would make his clothing and footwear by hand. In fact, his sandal design was unlike any other. It had a simple freedom of movement and proved wildly popular when brought to Europe and the United States.

Raymond Duncan believed that he saw the world in much the same way as did the ancient Athenians, especially Socrates, the philosopher. Socrates had spent his long life on the streets of Athens, teaching and questioning his fellow citizens, dressed in the simplest of togas. Like his ancient Greek hero, Raymond Duncan believed a person never could be accurately judged by his or her clothing and, therefore, never should be. Those who did so judge, he felt, were ignorant. Besides, for him, the toga was very practical, reliable, and effective in all kinds of weather.

To the end of his days, he disdained much of what others did. He understood, nevertheless, that the effect of such individuality led to a lonely journey through life. His sister Isadora, in her own way through dance, reflected a similar philosophy of life.

In 1903, the Duncans arrived in the ancient city, and their hearts were filled with excitement as they climbed the steps of the hill known as the Acropolis to the Parthenon, Athena's temple. Rather than feeling born again, Isadora Duncan felt born for the first time in the presence of such beauty.

The whole family was together again: Isadora, her mother,

and her three siblings. They looked upon the sunset and at each other, and decided right there that Greece was where their destiny would be fulfilled, together. Perhaps, they thought, they did not need the rest of the world. Perhaps the Duncan family was quite effective on its own. With the arrival of Augustin Duncan's graceful and beautiful wife and child, all felt, for the first time, in view of the Parthenon, perfect.

Isadora Duncan spent a good deal of her time in Athens studying ancient Greek art, especially the rhythm of the architecture, and she generated many new ideas for expressing with the human body her feelings about the beauty and harmony of the Greek columns. She felt a real connection between her involvement in body movement and the Greeks' appreciation of the human form. Everything she saw set inspiration soaring or tears flowing. She even gave a performance of an ancient Greek play to which she added her special dance movements. A chorus of Greek boys participated in the singing.

With money earned from her previous Berlin performances, Duncan and her family began creating their own "temple." They found a plot of land on another hill on the level of the Acropolis, in view of the temple of Athena. Once they gained ownership from the five families who owned the land, they set about the task of building their temple, from the first stone.

They used the modest red stone from the bottom of Mount Pontelicus, and each day these "holy" blocks were carried in carts up the tortuous paths. The foundation was properly blessed in a solemn ceremony attended by many people from the surrounding countryside, led by an old priest. At that point, the Duncans decided to stay in Greece forever. The connection between the ancient and pure beauty of Athens, the Acropolis, and the great Greek culture held them for some time. The attraction lasted until the real world intruded again and Isadora Duncan realized that their bank account was decreasing daily.

She went, one evening when sleep would not come, to the Acropolis alone. At the theater of Dionysus, she danced, she understood, for the final time in this country. "Suddenly it seemed to me as if all our dreams burst like a glorious bubble, and we were not, nor ever could be, other than moderns. We could not have the feeling of the Ancient Greeks. . . . The beautiful illusion of one year spent in Hellas seemed suddenly to break."

In three days, Greece would become their most recent memory, and Vienna their newest destination. They were accompanied by the chorus of Greek boys with whom the Duncans had performed in Athens and by the boys' priest professor who had performed with them.

Their time in Vienna in 1904 was spent on Isadora Duncan's art. Her performance at the Karl Theater there, with the chorus of Greek singers, was received with great applause. In a speech given right after a performance, Duncan explained that her goal was "to give the spirit of the Greek Tragedy." The cheering then began all over again.

In Munich, the chorus of Greek boys was, once again, successful. The boys were given rave reviews for their pure voices, and Isadora Duncan was praised for her grace and creativity in performing *On the Beautiful Blue Danube*.

In Berlin, especially at the weekly receptions at their home, Isadora Duncan's new form of dance was hotly debated. Duncan was always clear that she could never have anything to do with the ballet. "Every movement shocked my sense of beauty, and whose expression seemed to me mechanical and vulgar." Columns appeared almost daily in the papers, some praising her genius and others criticizing Isadora as the one who was destroying the real classic dance (the ballet). Also, at this time, the boys' voices began to change as they reached puberty. So Duncan regretfully sent them back to Athens.

More of Duncan's time was her own now, and she continued giving weekly receptions, which were attended by many in the artistic and literary world of Berlin. At one gathering, she met Karl Federn, a writer, who introduced her to the ideas of German philosopher and poet Friedrich Nietzsche. She was immediately drawn to Nietzsche, especially because, in his writings, he expressed the image of the wise man as a dancer and truth, when told, was light. He said, "Count that day lost in which you have not danced."

Duncan was so involved in her studies with Federn that she

47

found meeting her performing obligations more and more difficult. Her manager begged her to tour more, but she wouldn't listen. At this point, she preferred reading, dancing at student gatherings, and writing letters to scientists like Ernst Haeckel, the famous German biologist and philosopher who studied evolution. Maybe, she thought, his ideas would give her an even deeper understanding of dance.

In the two years since she had performed in Budapest, Duncan had been tightly focused on her art. Every part of her mind and body had been spent on Greek sculpture and ideas. At the start of the summer of 1904, however, Isadora Duncan began focusing on the music of Richard Wagner, the world-famous German composer. The year before, Wagner's widow, Cosima Wagner, had invited Duncan to perform in Bayreuth, Germany, at the Bayreuth Festival. There, under the art direction of Cosima Wagner, the music dramas of Richard Wagner were performed every year.

In Bayreuth, 27-year-old Isadora Duncan was without her family near her for the first time in a long while. Brother Raymond was back in Athens. Elizabeth Duncan and her mother were in Switzerland for the summer. Despite preparing for her Bayreuth performance, Duncan managed to find time for Heinrich Thode, an art historian with whom she fell in love. She had believed she could never feel this way except when dancing. Duncan could not eat or sleep.

Nevertheless, Duncan continued rehearsing her dances for Richard Wagner's opera *Tannhäuser*. After an argument with Cosima Wagner over the meaning she put into her dance of the Three Graces in the Bacchanal in *Tannhäuser*, Isadora Duncan came to understand more about the inner nature of dance. She explained to a cool Cosima Wagner that while drama was the spoken word, which came from logic, music expressed the passion belonging to the words. An easy union, which Cosima Wagner had suggested, between the music (and the dance), on one hand, and the words, on the other, seemed impossible. But they persevered.

Duncan saw the brain as the extra "energy of the body. The body, like an octopus, will absorb everything it meets and only give to the brain what it finds unnecessary to itself." In Isadora Duncan's view, the brain was not the center of our five senses. It was, instead, an organ that fed off the total energy of the body. That explained to her why dance was such a special art.

When Isadora Duncan finally performed the dance of the Three Graces in the Bacchanal of *Tannhäuser,* she caused a sensation, but this time not with her talent. Now it was with her costume, a sheer tunic, which showed all her dancing body. Cosima Wagner sent a long white robe to her, hoping she would wear it over her tunic. Duncan refused, declaring she would do things her way or not at all. Duncan, along with Mary Desti, even wore Greek-style tunics offstage, to dinner. Isadora Duncan then predicted, "You will see, before many years, all your Bacchantes and flower maidens will dress as I do." Cosima Wagner—seeing that Mary Desti also wore a tunic—asked Duncan if all Americans dressed like her, and Duncan dramatically replied, "Oh no, some wear feathers."

Debate raged about the modesty of wearing tights versus the beauty of the human body when inspired. For that time, Isadora Duncan's clothing was startling. Women often wore uncomfortable, tightly corseted outfits, and Isadora Duncan abandoned it all not only on stage but in everyday dress. Women, she felt, chose their clothes with the goal of attracting men. Duncan wanted her new ideas about fashion to help women to be natural, healthy, and intelligent, instead. These attributes she believed would, in the end, also attract men. And Isadora Duncan rarely had problems attracting men.

Isadora Duncan's love for Heinrich Thode was complicated by the fact that he was married at the time to Cosima Wagner's daughter. Duncan soon found that nothing could come of their feelings. Summer passed quickly, Thode left on a lecture tour, and Duncan went on a dance tour of Germany. Duncan decided to devote herself to a long-held dream: establishing her own school of dance. At the end of 1904, she bought a house in the Grünewald section of Berlin and began advertising for students as she simultaneously planned a dance tour of Russia.

At almost the same time, she met Edward Gordon Craig, son of actress Ellen Terry. Both she and Craig were spontaneous,

Isadora Duncan, Mary Desti, and Raymond's daughter in
Bayreuth, 1904.

ethereal people, and they fell in love almost immediately.

Therefore, when Isadora Duncan left for Russia, it was at an
uncomfortable time for her. Her love for Craig left her with no
appetite for food, lessened the energy behind her dance, and
caused her sleepless nights. She was touring alone in Russia and
could think of nothing except Edward Craig. She wished, in her
unhappiness, to be swallowed by the ice and snow of St.
Petersburg's winter. She felt—missing Craig and enduring the
frigid Russian winter—that the trip just wasn't worth the misery
involved.

CHAPTER SIX

The Russian Experience and the Isadora Duncan School of Dance in Germany

When Isadora Duncan came to St. Petersburg for the second time after a brief trip to Berlin to see Craig, she viewed the tragic funeral march for the many Russian workers shot down a few days before. In January 1905, they had committed the "crime" of taking part in a peaceful demonstration asking the czar, the Russian emperor, for economic reforms. Troops had opened fire and hundreds of people were killed and wounded. Duncan felt that seeing this horrible sight was fate, because the train had been 12 hours late. The experience changed her view of life. She promised herself that she and whoever she could influence would come to the aid of poor working people. She began to feel that unless her art could help these masses, it was useless.

Her performance for the wealthy of St. Petersburg soon after this tragic episode took on new importance. The passion that had been missing in her heart because of the pain over being apart from Edward Craig returned with a flourish. In what she described as a cobwebbed tunic, she danced to the music of Chopin with terrific energy. From the first, applause exploded and continued to the end.

Duncan even received a visit the next day from the great Russian ballerina Mathilde Kschessinskaya. She invited Duncan to a performance of the Russian Ballet at the Opera that very evening. Duncan was gratified by the friendliness. She arrived in a carriage right out of Cinderella's ball, though she still wore a white tunic and sandals. Despite her opposition to ballet as true art, she was quite taken by Kschessinskaya's "fairy-like figure . . . as she flitted across the stage, more like a lovely bird or butterfly than a human being."

Some nights later, she attended the ballet *Giselle*, upon invitation from Anna Pavlova, the leading dancer and one of Russia's greatest ballerinas. Again, despite her feelings about classical ballet, Isadora Duncan sat in a trance before such grace.

She dined later at Pavlova's house where she met Léon Bakst, the great Russian artist, who sketched her. It was a uniquely beautiful picture, her curls hanging down on one side. After that, Bakst, who was said to have some extrasensory powers, studied her hand. Years later, Duncan wrote that he had declared upon the discovery of two crosses in her palm, "You will have great glory, but you will lose the two creatures whom you love most on earth." At that moment, Duncan had no idea to what his grim prediction referred.

Her brief second visit to Russia ended because she had to fulfill previously made commitments to perform in Berlin in the spring. In spite of the brief time she was in Russia, she would be remembered. Isadora Duncan's artistic philosophy of dance was a constant source of discussion. In fact, one duel was actually fought over it. Her influence found its way into Russian ballet where Chopin and Schumann were played. Some ballet dancers even had the courage to take off their shoes and stockings to dance barefoot.

On her return to Berlin, Isadora continued the organization of her new dance school in the villa she had bought in Grünewald. She enlisted the enthusiastic help of her mother and her sister, Elizabeth.

To furnish the dream, she purchased 40 little

Russian artist Léon Bakst's sketch of Isadora Duncan.

beds, each covered with lovely white draperies held back with blue ribbons. It was to be a place made for children. Sculptures and artwork of children were placed around the villa. Duncan wanted to show the child's form as it was thought of by artists throughout history. She aimed to establish a connection between children across history and those in her school. She also wanted the children to become followers who would be inspired by her vision. As adults, they would help other children to experience the world of art. This understanding was symbolic of the new art of dance.

The statues and paintings of young girls placed all around the villa were meant to serve as models and ideals for the students to emulate and perhaps one day resemble. Each day, Isadora hoped every child would understand a little more of the special connection that could allow them to use the beauty to which they were exposed.

Duncan believed that gymnastics played a key part in the body's progress, "to draw out all the vital forces of the body towards its fullest development." Once done, dance could emerge from the spirit. Daily exercises were done to make the body "an instrument as perfect as possible . . . ready to flow into the being prepared for it."

Nature played an important part in movement study. What the wind did, how trees swayed, a bird's flight, the turning of leaves all would be reflected in how students would endow and enrich their movements with meaning. They would realize what made each movement special. All the parts of their flexible, growing bodies were to be trained to respond to their feelings. They would react to nature's tune and actively "sing" along with nature.

Although the villa was in Grünewald, Germany, the children who came there were among the poorest in the German cities. Many of the children had absentee or sick parents. Duncan declared she didn't really want rich children, for they had other opportunities to be exposed to art. She wanted the poor for what they could gain that they might otherwise never have. Duncan housed and taught them free of charge. She clothed them and provided basic necessities. She brought in a public school teacher to offer general academic work and took them to museums to add to their cultural growth. It was a dream for poor families to be given such an opportunity for their children, and it was accepted with gratitude. Isadora Duncan was in charge of the training, school administration was tended to by Elizabeth, and two governesses took care of the children. The school also arranged for its pupils to attend concerts and visit historic sites.

Isadora Duncan and her students at her school of dance in Grünewald, Germany, in 1905.

Auditions for admission to the school were informal and gentle. Acceptance was often offered on a feeling, a certain charm, or something in the eyes.

During its time, nearly 20 girls aged up to 10 were in the school. That's all she could afford to house and teach. When some left, new ones came in. Six remained throughout, and they would later become known as the Isadorables: Anna Denzler from Switzerland; Theresa Kruger and Elizabeth Milker of Dresden; Irma Erich-Grimme and Erica Lohmann from Hamburg; and Margot Gehle of Berlin.

Isadora Duncan's new ideas of education created much interest. All manner of professionals came to visit only to discover that these revolutionary ideas were not part of a new system. Simply, Duncan used her school to help children to progress individually, as people and students, at their own pace and in their own style. Visiting educators and other experts were impressed by the atmosphere of peace and the sense of culture that were everywhere. The girls' personalities were allowed to be fully natural and all visitors left charmed.

Elizabeth explained, when asked about such young children being treated as true artists, that none of them was being trained to be selfishly independent. "Each is but a link, a small link in a bewitching chain."

The girls loved Isadora Duncan. In fact, many worshipped her. The children felt appreciated, respected, and deeply cared for. They spoke of beautiful dreams they had at night about their "fairy queen."

However, once her success across Europe began to grow, Duncan's absences from the school were more frequent and longer. Sadly, since she was so revered by the children, the six originals were left especially heartbroken and feeling quite alone when she was away.

Besides her growing fame, there was another reason for separation: her romantic relationships. These caused the school, at times, to be at the bottom of her list of priorities. Yet, even with Duncan's inconsistent behavior, she did save her longest-lasting passion for her pupils. She always came back to them.

Elizabeth and Isadora Duncan were very different. Elizabeth,

Isadora Duncan and some of her students in Paris in 1908. The school in Germany had to close for financial reasons.

because of a chronic limp, did not dance. They also treated children very differently. Isadora lavished attention and hugs, while Elizabeth was more formal and perhaps somewhat distant. The combination, however, provided all that was needed.

Certainly, whenever Isadora Duncan was around, the atmosphere was more charged and alive. The children gave themselves over fully to her in class because she created happiness in them. There was mutual respect that was both rare and compelling.

From the start, the Grünewald school had money difficulties, and it always seemed on the edge of bankruptcy. Despite Isadora Duncan's impressive income, expenses were enormous. Admirers of her dancing and teaching methods set up a society in 1905 to help support the school through sponsoring performances, fund raising, and public relations in the business area. For the next three years, the students performed frequently, demonstrating the excellence of the school. Isadora Duncan joined them when she was able, but Elizabeth Duncan was the one who took care of the preparations and programs.

Although Elizabeth Duncan was not physically able to dance, she created dances for the children that were appropriate to their sizes and variety of abilities. She had the capacity to get the children to feel the music, and she understood the value of letting them discover where the movement would take them.

The students' performances were quite popular, although there always seemed to be some objection to the children's dancing barefoot in public. Yet, even with that, they went on to receive more rave reviews. They even impressed the English novelist and playwright John Galsworthy, who was moved to tears by the children. Of one, he wrote, "She danced as never child danced . . . full of the sacred fire of motion."

Financial problems, however, forced the Isadora Duncan School of the Dance at Grünewald to close in 1908. Some of the children returned to their families. Others, including the original six, the Isadorables, eventually moved with Elizabeth Duncan to Darmstadt, almost 200 miles away in southwestern Germany. There, Elizabeth Duncan set up her own dance school. The Isadorables taught younger students and bided their time until they might perform professionally themselves. In a break from her usual solo style, Isadora Duncan choreographed pieces that included the group of six.

The school's financial problems had been made worse by the demands of Duncan's stardom, her lack of general control over the workings of the school, and protests by some who did not believe children should perform in public. Many people also criticized Isadora's private life.

Isadora Duncan responded publicly to those who believed she was less than moral in her personal life. At Berlin's Philharmonic Hall, while lecturing on dance as an art of freedom, Duncan declared her theory of "the rights of a woman to love and bear children as she pleased." It was her opinion that a woman was free to select the father of her children, whether or not marriage was involved.

Response from the audience was swift. Half left, many threw things on the stage, and catcalls were heard from the audience. But she had made her point—and had declared her behavior her own responsibility.

CHAPTER SEVEN

Craig, Duse, and Deirdre

Part of Isadora Duncan's personal life that some people objected to was her relationship with the English actor, stage designer, and producer Edward Gordon Craig. He had come into her life at the end of 1904. Duncan was then 27 and Craig 32. He had seen her perform, found himself speechless, and immediately fell in love with her. Much later, when Craig was an old man, he remembered seeing a youthful Duncan in almost heavenly terms. "She was telling the air the very things we longed to hear and till she came we never dreamed we should hear; and now we heard them and this sent us all into an unusual state of joy."

A passionate love affair followed. She felt that Craig understood her mind in a way no one else ever had. The clearest result of their relationship was that Isadora Duncan found she was to become a mother.

She kept traveling, giving performances in Germany, Belgium, the Netherlands, Sweden, and then in Germany again. In between trips, she taught her devoted pupils at Grünewald between 1904-08. Craig went with her on some of her German tours. But as her pregnancy progressed, the traveling, especially by boat, made her very sick, and she decided to stop touring for the time being.

As if going back to some of her earliest memories, Duncan longed to return to the sea, alone. She rented a villa in Noordwijk on the North Sea coast of the Netherlands not far from The Hague. She hired a village doctor to care for her, but he was not used to anyone but the simple, poor women in the village.

Craig was there, on and off, but it was the child growing inside her that occupied her time. "It was strange to see my beautiful marble body softened and broken and stretched and deformed. It is an uncanny revenge of Nature, that the more refined the nerves, the more sensitive the brain, the more all this leads to suffering. Sleepless nights, painful hours. But joy too. Boundless, unlimited joy. . . ."

The loneliness of the sea called to her, and Isadora Duncan grew to love it again. She resented any intrusion from the outside. People's trivial comments irritated her. For the most part, the sea, the dunes, and the life inside her were her companions.

Her moods changed as often as the height of the waves. Though she struggled to maintain some balance, it was difficult. As apart as Duncan had become, she felt people wanted less and less to do with her. Craig was especially hard to deal with. He spent what seemed to be endless hours on his art—he was widely known for designing stage sets and producing plays—while hers held little interest at all for her. All Duncan could involve herself in was her condition, which she described as "this maddening, joy-giving, pain-giving mystery."

An endless summer passed, and Isadora Duncan grew larger and larger. Now, when it was nearly impossible, she thought of

English stage designer Edward Gordon Craig with Isadora Duncan in 1904.

dance more often. Yet, when the baby kicked and turned, she would smile, thinking, "After all, what is Art but a faint mirror for the Joy and Miracle of Life?" She felt limited by her body's changes, though, and was more miserable than joyous. Her fame seemed gone, her ambition destroyed. She felt incapable, at times like this, of dealing with the child to come.

Motherhood was sacred for Isadora Duncan. It was never a question of not wanting to have the baby, but she felt no one truly cared. Her mother had gone back to the United States, and she felt abandoned. She knew, as well, that her mother would never approve of a baby born outside marriage.

She also had to deal with her own morals, her sense of right and wrong. She had been very clear about that in her lectures. Now that she was to be the mother of an illegitimate child, she didn't know what to do. She even considered suicide. Gordon Craig, illegitimate himself, felt no need of marriage. In fact, he had left his wife and four children for an actress with whom he had a child. At the time Craig met Duncan, he had two other illegitimate children with another woman with whom he was in a serious relationship. More important for him than anything else, though, was his art.

Yet, the reality of Duncan's baby jolted her through its movements, and negative feelings, no matter how strong, disappeared. Finally, in late September, early labor arrived. If Duncan felt the previous nine months were hard to deal with, she had no clue to what was in store. With the first pain, "the torture began, as if I, poor victim, were in the hands of some mighty and pitiless executioner. . . . Talk about the Spanish Inquisition! No woman who's borne a child would have to fear it."

Labor battered her for two days and nights. "It is unheard of, uncivilized barbarism. . . . It should be remedied. It should be stopped." Not this time, though, and on the third day, forceps in hand, the doctor went to work.

To Duncan's surprise, she did not die. Although the embarrassment about the birth process she went through bothered her forever after, she experienced unspeakable joy when she saw her child, born on September 26, 1905.

"The baby was astonishing, formed like a Cupid, with blue

eyes and long, brown hair. . . . Now I know this tremendous love, surpassing the love of man. . . . I felt I was a God, superior to any artist." Duncan and Craig named her Deirdre, which in Irish means "beloved of Ireland."

During this period of forced rest, Isadora Duncan and Edward Gordon Craig were introduced by their neighbor, Juliette Mendelssohn, to one of Mendelssohn's idols—the famous Italian actress Eleanora Duse. They enjoyed each other's company greatly. Duse hired Craig to create the scenery for a production of the Norwegian poet and dramatist Henrik Ibsen's play *Rosmersholm* in Florence. Duncan, Craig, and Duse went to the Italian city by train, with Duncan happily nursing Deirdre and interpreting for the two artists so they would understand each other. Duse knew no English, and Craig understood no French or Italian. Duncan, in an effort to help them manage to get along, engaged in some interpreter's mischief. "I hope some of the lies which I told in interpreting may be forgiven me, for they were in a holy cause. I wanted this production to come off," she said, "and it would never have done so if I had really told Eleanora Duse what Craig said to her; and if I had repeated Duse's orders to Craig exactly as she expressed them."

This went on for some time. Duncan, despite her need to build her strength after Deirdre's birth, put herself in the middle of these two artists' explosive personalities. Once Craig was fully under way, she had to keep Duse out of his way tactfully, so the project could be completed. Craig was working to express his own vision for the scenery, and Duse was expecting something completely different. When he finished, Isadora Duncan escorted a tense and anxious Eleanora Duse to the theater.

When Craig had the curtain raised, they were speechless. Never had Duse seen such incredible beauty and vision. Duse held Duncan's hand tightly, hugged her, and stared silently, tears streaming down her face. Craig had achieved his masterpiece. Eleanora Duse was happy. Isadora Duncan sighed from the great relief of having succeeded at the interpreter's balancing act.

With this apparently successful partnership, Duncan pictured a bright future for Craig. Yet, it turned out that Eleanora Duse was performing in a repertory theater where there was a different play each night. All of Craig's work was spent on one night. Also, because of Eleanora Duse's fickle nature, their working connections suddenly soured.

On top of that, Duncan's bank account was almost empty. Two years of less than a full schedule of dance tours and performances, the expenses of the baby, her school, and the trip to Florence had all taken their toll. She needed money quickly, and in the nick of time, as 1906 ended, an offer came from Warsaw, Poland, asking if Isadora Duncan was ready to dance again. If she was, she could tour in Poland.

The journey was a sad one, though, for Duncan. It was her first time away from Deirdre, and her separation from Craig was difficult. Her health was not what she wanted it to be, and the baby was not fully weaned from mother's milk, so Duncan felt a sense of guilt about that. Deirdre was left in the care of a nurse in Italy, at San Remo.

Duncan's loneliness forced her to cut the Polish tour short, and she moved on to a tour in the Netherlands, which was closer to home. On stage in Amsterdam, she became ill with neuritis, which caused her to fall in and out of uncontrolled hysteria for weeks. Craig came for about a month to help in her recovery, but he left soon for Nice, France. Despite her condition, Isadora Duncan tried to follow him to Nice, but he was no longer there.

Duncan's mother came back, though, for a visit, and Deirdre was with her. However, her recovery proceeded slowly, and her mood did not brighten very much. Paying for the expenses of her family and her school continued to be a major problem, so Duncan decided to go on tour with some of the Grünewald pupils. In this way, perhaps government funding might somehow find its way to her school. So, after she had regained some of her strength, Duncan went on more dance tours of the Netherlands, Sweden, Switzerland, and Germany in 1907. Unfortunately, her pleas for government funding failed to gain financial help for her Grünewald school.

That same year, Duncan began to realize that her relationship with Craig was falling apart. When he was with her, she felt inferior to him. She was not near the spotlight of her art. He controlled her sense of herself through sheer force of his personality and genius. Duncan did not feel confident. She was no longer the center of attention. When he was gone, she was jealous of the women who constantly flirted with him. In any case, she couldn't work, dance, or care about her public.

After her breakup with Craig, Duncan needed reassurance. She found it when she went to St. Petersburg in December 1907 to give a series of concerts. She also traveled to Moscow, where she met Constantin Stanislavsky, director of the Moscow Art Theatre. They discussed dance theories, acting, how movements can show feelings, and how to remain passionate through many performances. This friendship made Duncan feel hopeful and positive again, even though it never developed into a love affair. Their friendship, deepened as it was by mutual respect, lasted a very long time.

Isadora Duncan was by this time world-renowned. Had she been able to settle for just being a star, her life might have been easier. But she still had dreams. She continued to believe in the idea of her dance school where she could touch lives. At times, she cursed her dreams, because they possessed her and never let her rest.

Yet she fought her negative thoughts and, between her dance recitals and tours, continued to teach her students. "Each day they grew stronger, more lithe, and the light of inspiration and divine music shone in their youthful forms and faces. The sight of these dancing children was so beautiful that it awakened the admiration of all artists and poets."

During her trip to Russia in late 1907 and early 1908, Duncan danced in St. Petersburg and Moscow where audiences appreciated her art. But some important composers objected to her dancing to serious music not specifically composed for dancing. Furthermore, the Imperial Ballet was so rooted in Russia, that no Russian financial support for her dance school came her way. Duncan understood that the time was not yet ripe for a school of free dance movement in Russia.

She decided next to try performing in England to get support for her school. In mid-1908, Isadora Duncan and some of her pupils gave several weeks of performances at the Duke of York Theatre in London. No aid emerged. High expenses forced

Duncan to return to Grünewald, Germany. She then signed a contract with the American theatrical manager Charles Frohman for an American tour. Isadora made arrangements for Deirdre to stay with her sister, Elizabeth, in Paris. Again she would feel the pain of separation from Deirdre, now almost one. She would also be putting thousands of miles between herself and Craig, with whom she still wanted to reconcile. Her pupils would be under the care of a governess in a house not too far from the French capital.

This was to be Isadora Duncan's first return to her native land since she and her mother, sister, and brothers had left it in 1899. Isadora Duncan had been an unknown when she left and she was coming back having become a famous star in Europe. She now wondered what her reception would be like in the United States.

Duncan traveled to England in 1908 to perform and seek support for her school.

CHAPTER EIGHT

New York, Paris, and Patrick

Isadora Duncan returned in the summer of 1908 to the United States almost nine years after she had left it. She had accomplished much in that time, she thought. She "was already famous in Europe . . . had created an Art, a School, a Baby. Not so bad. But, as far as finances went, was not much richer than before."

When she danced her Greek-inspired dances before audiences in New York City that August, their response was not very favorable. Charles Frohman, usually an effective manager, had not promoted her as a serious dancer. Instead, he presented her as a popular Broadway attraction, which she was not.

Despite the financial failure, and Frohman's advice to return to Europe because Americans could not understand her art, Duncan hung on. After a performance one night, she met the famous American sculptor George Grey Barnard. He encouraged her, wanted to create a sculpture in her image, and gave her hope. She rented a studio in the New York City, created new work, and danced every evening for poets and artists.

Her circle then included the poets Edwin Arlington Robinson, Ridgely Torrence, and William Vaughn Moody; the painters George Bellows and Robert Henri; and the young writer Max Eastman. The general public did not fully appreciate her, but artists like these certainly did.

A review by the critic Mary Fanton Roberts in an art magazine, expressed the sentiments of her special audience. In part, Roberts wrote, "It is far back, deep down the centuries, that one's spirit passes when Isadora Duncan dances; back to the very morning of the world, when the greatness of the soul found free expression in the beauty of the body, when rhythm of motion corresponded with rhythm of sound, when the movements of the human body were one with the wind and sea."

This review came at just the right time, for Duncan had been dealing with audiences that didn't seem to care about what she was doing. Most of the critics who viewed her then didn't understand or appreciate her art. They had announced that Isadora Duncan could never succeed in the United States. So Roberts's kind words gave Duncan hope, and the two became close friends.

One result of the few favorable reviews was a visit by conductor Walter Damrosch, who was the director of the New York Symphony Orchestra. He proposed a series of dances for Duncan at the Metropolitan Opera House for late in the year. With a world-famous orchestra of 80, conducted by Damrosch himself, Duncan was truly motivated. She danced to the music of Beethoven's *Seventh Symphony*. Later she danced to Gluck's *Iphigenia at Aulis*. The performances were great triumphs. It was as if she were a center point used to express the emotional feeling of the music.

Duncan and the orchestra toured the United States, performing in Boston, Washington, D.C., and other cities. At least professionally, this was probably the happiest Isadora Duncan had been in her life. She missed Deirdre, of course, but now there was great hope, a future with a strong foundation.

Even President Theodore Roosevelt, who saw her perform in Washington, D.C., reacted to protests of some church leaders against Duncan's dance. "What harm can these Ministers find in Isadora's dances? She seems to me as innocent as a child dancing through the garden in the morning sunshine and picking the beautiful flowers of her fantasy."

It had become quite interesting to see how people in the United States reacted to Duncan. Like a troublemaker, she caused talk wherever she went. Duncan rather liked the commotion she created and always felt she was simply exercising her rights of free speech and expression.

Her financial condition had temporarily improved by the end of the tour. She was eager to return to Deirdre and the school. She left the United States at the end of December 1908 and sailed back to Europe. Duncan was still without a backer for her school, which cost her $10,000 a year to operate. To make matters worse, when she evaluated her financial situation it was clear that the tour losses in August had turned her later profits of November and December into losses.

On Isadora's return to Paris, in early 1909, Elizabeth brought Deirdre and 20 of her students to greet her. It had been a long six months and both her loves—her little baby who had grown and her pupils—were joys to behold.

She performed soon after her return, managed by Aurélian-Marie Lugné-Poe, the French actor and theatrical manager. He also represented the actress Eleanora Duse and the playwright Henrik Ibsen. Lugné-Poe understood the setting needed for Duncan's dance, and audiences in Paris, like those in the United States, went wild.

Although she had closed her school in Grünewald, Germany, the previous summer, the number of pupils in France was growing. Her school in Paris now covered two floors of an apartment building at No. 5 rue Danton. Deirdre, not surprisingly, was running from room to room and dancing freely.

Yet in spite of all this happiness and all her adoring fans, she was worried. The

This poster of Isadora Duncan may have been created by the Dutch artist Kees van Dongen.

expenses of her growing school had strained Duncan's finances to the breaking point. She had cared for and educated 40 children, 20 in Germany and 20 in Paris. She joked that a millionaire had to be found for the school to continue, and in fact, this did become an obsessive search.

The morning after an evening performance, Duncan was notified by her maid, who was carrying a visiting card, that a gentleman was calling. She glanced at the name and declared to herself, "Here is my millionaire!"

To her maid, she simply said, "Let him enter."

In came Paris Eugene Singer. Duncan would always call him Lohengrin after the knight of the swan, the hero of an old German legend who saves a noble lady in distress. Singer was tall, blond, and bearded. "You do not know me, but I have often applauded your wonderful art," he said.

He was 41 years old, a man of easy friendliness with a kind of royal attitude. In fact, his father, Isaac Merritt Singer, had been an American inventor who had patented an improved sewing machine and had made millions of dollars manufacturing it. Isaac Merritt Singer had moved to England where he died when Paris was a young boy. Paris's sisters married French aristocrats. In fact, one of his sisters was Princess de Polignac for whom Duncan had performed concerts eight years earlier. Paris had been raised as a ward of the British court. He was very rich, which allowed him to express his generosity often. Paris Eugene Singer loved to do things on a grand scale, and that agreed exactly with Isadora Duncan's own ideas.

His conversation continued, "I admire your art, your courage in the ideal of your school. I have come to help you. Would you like, for instance, to go with all these dancing children to a little villa on the Riviera, by the sea, and there compose new dances? The expense you don't need to worry about. I will bear it all. You have done a great work; you must be tired. Now let it rest on my shoulders."

At the villa, the children in their tunics were free to dance amid the beautiful scenery of Beaulieu on the coast of the Mediterranean Sea in southern France. They were treated with great kindness by Singer. He, in turn, was regarded by Duncan as a knight in shining armor. Singer was, in her view, unapproachable, yet so very giving. This worshipful feeling bloomed into love when Singer showed deep concern at the sudden illness of the school's youngest child, Erica.

Then, on a sudden whim, after Erica's recovery, Duncan and Singer left on his yacht with Deirdre and sailed to Italy. The school was left in the care of governesses.

Isadora Duncan had often been suspicious of wealth because she feared too much of it could only bring sadness. Her association with the millionaire Singer tested her theory. Despite his giving nature, Singer was, as he seemed when Duncan first met him, little more than a child, very spoiled and unready for her revolutionary ideas. This was confirmed one night in a heated discussion over favorite poems. When she declared that "Song of the Open Road" by the great American poet Walt Whitman was her favorite, Singer was disgusted. Here are a few lines of the poem:

> From this hour I ordain myself loosed of limits and
>   imaginary lines,
> Going where I list, my own master total and absolute,
> Listening to others, considering well what they say,
> Pausing, searching, receiving, contemplating,
> Gently, but with undeniable will, divesting myself of
>   the holds that would hold me
> I inhale great draughts of space,
> The east and west are mine, and the north and south
>   are mine.

"What rot!" Singer exclaimed. "That man could never have earned his living!"

"Can't you see," Duncan cried, "he had the vision of Free America?"

"Vision be damned!"

He saw factories where she saw openness. Thus, even though she loved him, she became uneasy. For example, Duncan was uncomfortable at his spending great sums to pay 50 sailors to operate the yacht for the pleasure of 3 people.

It wasn't that money was of no use to her. She spent much of

Isadora Duncan with her daughter Deirdre and her son Patrick.

her life working for it or asking or almost begging for it. Money was, however, something to be used, not hoarded. She believed that great wealth, which was appealing, should have a noble purpose. For her, that was to build a great theater for the dance. It was to establish schools everywhere for children—to nurture their spirits, stir their imaginations, and make them strong.

Duncan, Singer, and Deirdre had to return to the French capital in the late spring of 1909 because of Duncan's previous agreements to give dance performances. Her musical accompaniment was directed by the famous French violinist and conductor Edouard Colonne and performed by his Colonne Orchestra. Once again, her dancing was met with enthusiasm.

Next, Duncan went on another short tour in Russia where she performed in Moscow and Kiev. While in Russia she met Craig who was working on stage sets for the Moscow Art Theatre. But their love affair was not rekindled.

Isadora Duncan came back to Paris. She accepted Singer's rich lifestyle or, at least, was hypnotized by it. She responded to the taste of fine food and the genius of a good dressmaker. Paul Poiret, the French dress designer, influenced by her Greek-inspired dance tunics, made some of her fashionable clothes. Duncan had purchased a big house and studio in Neuilly-sur-Seine near Paris and was busy having the place decorated. Her concern with the poor people of the world faded for a while, as she took pleasure in being served. She liked the way waiters treated Singer and her. His generous tipping policy, in fact, guaranteed good service, because he did so before the meal—not after.

Yet Singer, for all his outward energy and joy, was often haunted by the vision of his dead mother in her coffin. He wondered aloud at the use of living. Duncan fully realized that money, regardless of how much one has, truly does not bring happiness. She spent that summer with him on his yacht off the northwest coast of France. In September, she journeyed to Venice, Italy, with Deirdre and the nurse, spending time with them alone.

One day, while in Venice's Cathedral of St. Marco, Duncan was struck by the vision of "a little boy, but also the face of an angel with great blue eyes and an aureole of golden hair." The vision caused her indecision and anguish. She was pregnant. Her dreams had risen so often to dizzying heights and realities, only to be shelved or postponed by life's events. Joyous as it was to have Deirdre, Duncan thought often of her pregnancy and worried about her ability to be unselfish again, delaying her hopes in other areas.

Duncan did seek medical advice. The doctor suggested that it might be best if she did not bring another life into a cruel world or deprive others of her art again. She also had to decide if she was ready to give birth to a child whose father could not overcome his selfish habits. She spent some time alone, then summoned the doctor and informed him of her decision. Duncan next returned to Deirdre and tenderly told her that she would

Isadora Duncan and Paris Eugene Singer.

have a new brother or sister within a few months.

Singer was delighted at the news. When he was informed as well that Duncan was to work again in the United States with Walter Damrosch, he excitedly agreed to go with her. It would be his first trip to the United States.

The tour began with favorable reviews in Philadelphia. There her grace was applauded and she was supported against a protest group of Sunday school teachers who were declared to be examples of the greatest obstacle to artistic growth in America. This understanding greatly heartened her and held her in Cleveland where, however, her dancing was condemned by Dr. Fayette L. Thompson, pastor of the Lidell Avenue Methodist Episcopal Church. He said her show was worse than burlesque and called the police. Yet, he had never actually seen her perform, and society women of St. Louis fired back in Duncan's defense. One of them declared, "Only an obscene mind could see anything vulgar in Isadora Duncan's dance." The tour remained happy, with rave reviews and money aplenty, until Duncan's pregnancy became too obvious for the tour to continue.

At the beginning of 1910, Singer and Duncan went on an extended vacation in Egypt. It included visits to ancient ruins and temples and a cruise up the Nile River. When they returned to Europe, Duncan spent much of her time at the Beaulieu villa in southern France, in the garden by the sea, thinking. She found herself wondering "if a woman can ever really be an artist, since Art is a hard task-master who demands everything, whereas a woman who loves gives up everything to life."

Despite Duncan's inner conflict, her son, Patrick, was born on May 1, 1910. Her second time in childbirth was far less painful than her first. This time she was tended to by a doctor who gave her morphine to deaden the pain. Deirdre came to see her mother, and her first comment showed a growing maternal side. According to Isadora Duncan's account, written years later, Deirdre had said, "Mother, you need not worry about him. I will always hold him in my arms and take care of him." These were not words that should have concerned her, but they did. As she looked at her two children, however, she could not explain why.

Restlessness stirred in Isadora Duncan again. She realized

once more that she was not meant for the home life. Duncan rededicated herself to her art. Though dance was a constant challenge, it was always more satisfying, in her view, than human beings. She gave dance recitals and spent some time at Paignton, Singer's huge estate in England. There she worked on choreographing dances for music by Gluck.

In early 1911, Isadora Duncan traveled once again to the United States. Her dance tour included performances at Carnegie Hall in New York City where Walter Damrosch conducted the New York Symphony Orchestra. She also performed in Boston; Washington, D.C.; and St. Louis. The tour gave Duncan a chance to appeal for funds for her school. Her determination was renewed by her experience with the life of the rich. She believed that such a life was without hope, that it was empty and selfish. It reinforced her belief that there can be no joy except in complete and free communication of feelings.

Drawing of Isadora Duncan by the Spanish artist José Clará.

Duncan's pleas for money had, therefore, a point of view new to many wealthy patrons of the arts. It took them by surprise because they were used to being listened to not scolded and lectured. Duncan's fund-raising methods went beyond the traditional—which should have surprised no one. "Of course I love America," she declared to one American audience.

> Why, this School, these children, are we not all
> the spiritual offspring of Walt Whitman. . . . It has

73

come from America, it is the dance of the America of the future.

Beethoven and Schubert were children of the people all their lives. They were poor men, and their great work was inspired by and belongs to Humanity. The people need great drama, music, dancing.

We went over the [Lower] East Side [at that time an immigrant neighborhood of crowded tenements] and gave a performance for nothing . . . and the people sat there transfixed, with tears rolling down their cheeks; that is how they cared for it.

Build a simple, beautiful theatre. You don't need to gild it. . . . Fine art comes from the Human Spirit and needs no externals. In our School we have no costumes, no ornaments—just the beauty that flows from the inspired human soul, and the body that is its symbol. . . . Beauty is to be looked for and found in our children; in the light of their eyes and in the beauty of their little hands outstretched in their movements. . . . These are my pearls and my diamonds! I want no others. Give beauty and freedom and strength to the children. Give art to the people who need it. Great music should no longer be kept for the delight of a few cultured people, it should be given free to the masses; it is as necessary for them as air and bread, for it is the Spiritual Wine of Humanity.

This trip to the United States was filled with happy and purposeful times, yet her return to Paris, France, was unforgettable. Isadora Duncan had left Patrick in a cradle and greeted a little boy running happily toward her.

CHAPTER NINE

Tragedy and Recovery

Isadora Duncan spent most of 1912 in France at her house and studio in Neuilly. At that time, Singer planned to have a special theater built for her in Paris. There, great actors such as Eleanora Duse would perform and Edward Gordon Craig would design the sets. But disagreements arose, and after one of his arguments with Duncan, Singer dropped plans for the theater. In early 1913, Isadora Duncan completed another strenuous Russian tour. By this time, she dreaded any more separations from her children. At home in Neuilly, Deirdre could be seen composing her own dances and moving rhythmically to poems she wrote. Duncan could overhear her daughter's voice sometimes saying, "Now I am a bird, and I fly so, so high among the clouds." With great pride, she dreamed that one day Deirdre would follow her in running the school.

Patrick was also involved in dance, working to a strange music all his own. Duncan could not teach him, for he announced, "No, Patrick will dance Patrick's own dance alone."

With this, her own studio dancing, and playing with her children, Duncan was content. Her ties to them, now both by birth and dance, grew stronger daily. She was part of them in every way. She viewed them with a mother's unconditional love and the inner joy of the artist.

As March arrived, Duncan gave dance performances in Paris with the girls known as the Isadorables. They had been her pupils five years earlier at her Grünewald school. They had traveled from Elizabeth Duncan's dance school in Darmstadt, Germany. In April, Isadora Duncan gave other concerts and recitals that met with acclaim. Nevertheless, she suffered from a sense of doom. One night, while dancing to Chopin's "Funeral March," she said, "I felt over my forehead that icy breath and smelt the same strong scent of white tuberoses and funeral flowers."

These omens were, for Isadora Duncan, like a "Prelude to a Tragedy," that shattered her peaceful life forever. She was to say, later, "One's body may drag along its weary way on earth, but one's spirit is crushed—for ever crushed. I have heard people speak of the ennobling influence of sorrow. I can only say that those last few days of my life, before the blow fell, were actually the last day of my spiritual life."

She kept having visions, often at night, sometimes with hooded figures, in black, looking at her with pleading eyes. A doctor diagnosed her problem as overstrained nerves, and he recommended rest. She decided to go with her children to nearby Versailles.

They packed and went. Duncan danced there, as well, and felt she had escaped the terrors of the recent past. She later recalled that she danced as never before, fiery and full of joy. Her passions now alive again, she was further surprised by a visit, after a performance, by Singer. She had not seen him in months. That night she had the soundest sleep in a very long time.

Morning arrived with Deirdre and Patrick jumping on her bed, giggling and laughing. They ate breakfast together, and Duncan noted that her son was even more active than usual.

She seized the opportunity, and with the nurse making a quartet, they danced together wildly, laughing joyously. Their moment was interrupted by the phone. It was Singer, asking to see the children, whom he hadn't been with in four months. Duncan had yearned for a reconciliation and was delighted at this visit.

The children were excited and wondered aloud where they might be going. The nurse, ever careful, broke in. "Madame, I think it's going to rain—perhaps they had better stay here."

The warning was said with instinctive kindness, but Duncan would not listen. She thought the nurse was being overprotective.

On April 19, they left for Paris, and as they drove, Duncan held her children tenderly. She was filled with hope for a renewed future with her Lohengrin, her pet name for Singer. He was thrilled to see the children, both of whom he loved deeply.

They ate Italian food for lunch and spoke of a theater to be built for them. Once done, Duncan realized she had to rehearse for an upcoming engagement, and Singer left. The nurse decided that the children should not stay at the Neuilly studio, for she felt they should return to Versailles to rest. As the children left, they kissed the glass of the back window of the car and their mother did the same where their lips touched. The cold remained on her lips as they drove away.

Duncan sat in the huge Neuilly dance studio, waiting for the rehearsal to begin. She went upstairs to the apartment she had there and thought about the happiness she felt: "My art, success, fortune, love, but above all, my beautiful children."

It was this daydream that was shattered by a noise she had never heard before. Stunned, she turned. Before her, barely able to stand, was Paris Singer. He fell in an eerie slow-motion faint-like drop and could say only these words: "The children—the children—are dead!"

Duncan was still, but her throat burned as if on fire. The news made no sense, and she quietly said so. It could not be true. But it was. The car that was taking the children back to Versailles was not far from the studio when the driver saw a taxi coming head-on. To avoid a crash, the driver stopped the car suddenly, and the engine stalled. The car had been going uphill, and the driver for safety's sake meant to leave the car in gear but accidentally clicked it into reverse. He left the car to crank the motor from the front. As he did so, the motor started again, and the limousine began sliding backward. The driver could only stare in horror as the car sped down, nothing to block its path, and plunged deep into the Seine River.

There were several witnesses, and they dove into the water, but they could not help. The police had to raise the car. Deirdre and the nurse were already dead, but Patrick held onto life by a thread. Tragically, all efforts by the doctor at the nearby American Hospital to save him were in vain.

When Isadora Duncan's close friend Mary Desti got to the hospital, she went directly to the morgue. On a marble slab lay the two children. She looked at them closely and tried to will them to breathe. She could not believe they were gone, but behind her, the doctor's voice could be heard. "It's too late. We have done everything."

Duncan could never really explain her reaction or what she felt, but she remembered that "when I felt in mine those little cold hands that would never again press mine in return, I heard my cries—the same cries as I had heard at their births. Why the same? Since one is the cry of supreme joy and the other of sorrow. I do not know why, but I know they are the same. Is it not that in all the universe there is but one great cry containing Sorrow, Joy, Ecstasy, Agony—the Mother Cry of Creation?"

She considered, then, shuddering, the traditional Christian burial and could not let it happen to her children. Isadora Duncan had almost always rebelled against what everyone else did. She hated organized religion and certainly did not agree with modern marriage customs. She refused to have her children baptized when they were born, and she would reject what was considered usual in their deaths.

Her one desire was to create beauty from the tragedy. She could not weep. She did not wear black. She later wrote that many traditionally religious people considered her "a heartless and terrible woman" simply because she "wanted to say farewell to my loved ones in Harmony, Colour, Light and Beauty, and because I brought their bodies to the Crematorium instead of putting them in the earth. . . . How long must we wait before more intelligence will prevail among us in Life, in Love—in Death?"

Isadora Duncan returned to Neuilly, France, and her studio. She felt, then, that she couldn't go on, that her life had no purpose or value without her children. Yet, it was then that the words of her other children, her pupils, jolted her: "Isadora, live for us. Are we not also your children?" That brought Duncan's self-pity to a stop, for there were grieving children to attend to.

Yet clearly her sorrow was deep, and her recovery was not helped by Singer, who did not respond to her need despite his personal grief. She was haunted as well by Deirdre's excited voice the day she learned of his visit, and the nurse's gentle warning to keep the children in on that fateful day.

Isadora Duncan remembered that for months before the accident there had been omens. Why hadn't she listened to them. She had once been told by a clairvoyant, one who supposedly could see into the future, that she would lose those most dear to her.

For Isadora Duncan, that tragedy ended any chance for a natural, happy life. Her main wish then was to flee from the horror of it all. She felt the need to be an invisible ship forever sailing an undiscovered ocean.

She did manage to send a thank-you message, printed in a newspaper, to those who had written to her after the tragedy. It said: "My friends have helped me to realize what alone could comfort me. That all men are my brothers, all women are my sisters and all little children on earth are my children."

In Paris, Isadora Duncan busied herself responding to all those who had supported her. Her public image—as a person remaining strong despite overwhelming tragedy—was impressive. Away from the public eye, however, everything simply fell apart. She no longer seemed to have a purpose in life. Her pain seemed endless as she faced the world alone. Her depression was total.

Yet, she did find some sense of purpose later in 1913: Duncan joined in helping starving children in war-torn Albania. This was a project in which her brother Raymond and his Greek wife Penelope were deeply involved. The First Balkan War, between Bulgaria, Serbia, Montenegro, and Greece on one side and Turkey on the other, had just ended. The suffering in Albania was great. Isadora Duncan viewed much tragedy firsthand. Just one of the hundreds of incidents she saw was that of a mother and her four children, all huddled together, under a tree, homeless. Their house had been burned down, husband and father killed by the Turks, crops ruined. The rescue group distributed sacks of potatoes to help the war victims keep hunger at bay and tools to help them rebuild their shattered homes and livelihoods.

Isadora, Raymond, and Penelope lived in a tent on a coastal mountainside. Sometimes, as they gave out supplies, the frequent thunderstorms drenched them. Isadora was at such moments thrilled by nature's unpredictable behavior.

Duncan returned to France exhausted, yet with a somewhat renewed spirit, better health, and a little happiness. Couldn't she, even though her beloved children were gone, live for others who needed her? But she came to realize, during another trip to

Albania, that she alone could not halt the misery of the people. She could no longer bear staying there. Yet she planned to continue to publicize the problems in Albania and to raise money to help the refugees there.

Isadora left Albania a second time and headed with Penelope to Constantinople. She spent her days thinking and resting. An urgent telegram brought them back once again to that poverty-stricken country. Raymond was ill with a serious fever. She tried to convince him to leave, but nothing could persuade him to do so. When she finally felt that he'd recover, she left for Switzerland. But there her depression resumed and could not be lifted. Even a visit by her brother Augustin changed nothing. Isadora finally returned to her studio in Neuilly, and for the first time since she learned of her children's deaths, she cried. Isadora imagined that she saw her children everywhere and heard their voices. She wept uncontrollably. With their belongings about as constant reminders, she could no longer stay there.

Duncan sped off in her car as quickly as possible. She crossed the Alps into Italy and simply drove around aimlessly.

One day, as she rested in a small Italian town near the sea, she received a telegram from her friend the actress Eleanora Duse, who had somehow tracked her down. Duse asked Duncan to visit her so she could comfort her. Isadora Duncan ran to her car and left immediately for Viareggio, an Italian seaside resort town.

As soon as Duncan arrived and saw her friend, she knew she had made the right decision. Duse not only held her and consoled her but also allowed her the time to grieve. That was something Duncan had felt she didn't have the right to do until then. Eleanora asked Isadora to talk about Deirdre and Patrick. She encouraged her to tell everything over and over. For the first time since her children's tragic deaths, Isadora felt she was not alone.

Duse also encouraged Duncan to return to dance, declaring it was her only way to survive. She pushed her to accept a contract offer in South America so Duncan could escape from the tragedy and aimlessness of life as it was then. Yet Duncan could not. It seemed to her impossible to go before the public again. She was still too vulnerable, too tortured. She felt secure alone with Eleanora Duse.

One afternoon, as Duncan walked along the beach still experiencing visions of Deirdre and Patrick, she literally felt herself going mad. With additional images of life in a mental institution, she fell onto the sand and cried bitterly.

Into this world of despair from which she had found no way out, there came a telegram from Paris Singer. It begged Duncan to return to the French capital for her art's sake. For that purpose she went.

Singer, too, was still deeply pained by the children's deaths. "I came to you first . . . to help you," he said after some difficulty, "but our love led us to tragedy. Now let us create your School, as you wish it, and some beauty on this sad earth for others." In January 1914, he had purchased a large mansion, a former hotel and restaurant, in Bellevue in order to make this happen. The building and its surrounding gardens were located on the edge of Paris. The palacelike building had rooms for as many students as she wanted and Isadora Duncan could only say yes. It was right and it was beautiful. The possibilities were breathtaking. By the next morning she was immersed in turning the hotel into a "Temple of the Dance of the Future."

Paris Singer's offering was named Dionysion. The original six girls, the Isadorables, were the first to come, and they were just as excited as Isadora Duncan. They had been studying and teaching at Elizabeth Duncan's dance school in Darmstadt. The new building in Bellevue was much larger than Isadora Duncan's first studio in Grünewald. Dionysion would serve perfectly as both a place to live and a school. Those selected to live there immediately brought positive energy to the huge mansion. They awakened a grieving Isadora Duncan into purpose again.

Within this beautiful building Duncan began to teach again, and the children learned quickly, with great enthusiasm. The famous sculptor Auguste Rodin lived close by and visited the school often. He sketched the young girls as they danced. He once noted that even though Duncan had had beautiful models to sketch in the past, these pupils were beyond his wildest dreams. Never had he met ones who understood and valued the body's movement as her students did.

Bellevue welcomed artists. Duncan believed that discussion

Isadora Duncan at Dionysion, her Bellevue mansion, given to her
by Paris Eugene Singer.

between them and her students could only enhance their experience. The artists loved the freedom they had to draw the girls in
all performing or studying activities. The students, for their part,
learned a great deal from these talented people.

Saturday was a free day for the pupils, though they often
danced during their free times. When not dancing, they could be

seen running through the woods, giggling, yelling, and playing games. Artists were sketching all the while.

Isadora Duncan ran this school in the same way as she did the others. No payment was expected for the time spent there. She asked only to borrow the students' imaginations, energies, and hearts for the period.

In 1914, the school gave a festival at the Trocadéro in Paris. Isadora Duncan carefully watched not only her students' performance but also the audience's reaction. "At certain parts of the program," she noted, "the audience rose and shouted with enthusiasm and joy. At the close they applauded at such length that they would not leave . . . this extraordinary enthusiasm for children who were in no wise trained dancers or artists, was enthusiasm for the hope of some new movement in humanity which I had dimly foreseen."

This concert was important to those who supported Duncan. It appeared, now, that the art Duncan was creating was not a fad or a trend. It was permanent. It could now begin to move from generation to generation, and the Isadorables became the way to spread this understanding. Thus, despite the pain that could never truly go away, Duncan found she was not depressed or melancholy at all. She managed to find the inner strength to teach almost every day. Even she had to marvel at what she appeared to be accomplishing. It was as if she "opened a way by which the spirit of the Dance flowed over them."

CHAPTER TEN

War Years

During the summer of 1914, Duncan felt a change happening. She called it "a strange oppression," and this feeling seemed to be everywhere. In reality, the world was soon to experience a monumental change in the form of world war.

It was not only that Duncan, in her effort, once more, to bring life into the world, was pregnant. It was not only the worry she felt because the movements within her were weaker than those of Deirdre and Patrick had been. She was tired, and Singer suggested an August vacation for the students and a rest for the teacher. The children traveled to England where they stayed at Singer's estate. Her friend Mary Desti and her brother Augustin stayed with Isadora. But once the children had left, Isadora's depression grew deeper, because her feeling of impending danger was growing more ominous—not only from within but from without.

She also knew this was the end of the Bellevue school after only seven months. It had given light to her darkness, but the oncoming reality of war made the ending of her beloved school seem almost unimportant, an early casualty of the approaching conflict.

To Isadora Duncan, it all seemed such a waste. That this institution, financially secure and wonderful in its beauty, would not last, was a tragedy. Art was eternal for her, wars were not. Yet, they always seemed to be around to destroy more than people realized.

Her fears were confirmed when in June—on the same day that her pupils gave the school's first public performance at the Trocadéro—headlines announced the assassination of Austria's archduke. War now seemed a certainty. The artistic rebirth she had been working so hard to bring to light now faded before the growing military tensions that would soon become world war.

At that time the nations of Europe were engaged in serious

competition for raw materials and for places to sell their manufactured goods. Some countries succeeded, but at the expense of others. Many workers labored in factories making warships and weapons, and bankers were searching for investment opportunities. Germany and Great Britain had become the major powers, and the area of struggle grew wider. Great Britain, Russia, and France allied on one side against Germany, Austria-Hungary, and Turkey on the other. An evil spirit spread across Europe—a feeling that pulled people apart.

With this threatening military situation came August and the onset of Isadora Duncan's labor. On August 3, Germany declared war on France. A thought came to Duncan that her baby would be a boy, but at least he would be too young to go to war.

Labor continued, and her baby was born. His cry brought tears of joy to Duncan, especially given all her earlier fears. When she held him, everything else faded to dust. The fear of war didn't matter, because she had her son. She allowed herself that bit of selfishness. Duncan knew about the great suffering that was beginning, but she gave herself this short, happy time.

Night came and she continued to rejoice as she held her baby. Without warning, he started gasping for air and his lips turned cold. Duncan called the nurse, who took the child as a clear emergency was at hand. She called for oxygen and anything else needed to deal with the problem.

One hour passed, an endless wait. Augustin finally came in with the news that Isadora Duncan had heard before and was certain she'd never hear again.

"Poor Isadora—your baby—has died."

Deirdre had died. Patrick had died. Now this third still-unnamed child was dead. The first two, it seemed to Isadora, were dying all over again. She watched as her friend Mary Desti took the cradle away to be used as the tiny coffin.

In the middle of this scene, a friend came in and spoke of everybody's losses, and the need to put individual sorrow aside. Duncan decided then and there to lend Bellevue to the French government to be used as a hospital center for Allied wounded.

The enthusiasm among the people for this war, the powerful sense of purpose, was everywhere. Even artists were ready to limit their usual statements about the value of art because now valuable human lives were being lost. In her heart, Duncan knew otherwise, though. Art was never less than vital, but she was swept along as she allowed her school to be used for others to recover.

As she saw firsthand, the dancing room was filled with cots for those who needed them. Her library was now an operating room. She knew it was necessary. Nevertheless, she also looked with horror at a place like this, "an academy for the higher life inspired by philosophy, poetry and great music," housing the tragedy of war.

When she was feeling physically somewhat better, Duncan, along with Mary Desti, went through war-torn areas in France, where they were treated with great respect. This expression of esteem was an honor Duncan hadn't expected and was quite thrilled at receiving.

Eventually, without Bellevue, she was forced to live elsewhere for a time. Because she was still too weak to travel, she rented a furnished villa, which was named "Black and White" because of its color scheme. She became depressed all over again. Away from Bellevue, her students, and their energy, she was all alone and helpless, though by her beloved sea. The seaside could provide little peace, because she was too weak to enjoy her usual walks by it.

She was without purpose and could not free herself from this emotionally depressed and physically weakened state. She asked for a doctor to come to her from the nearby military hospital, but he refused to make the medical visit to her. Finally, she visited the doctor at the hospital and was given this prescription: "Only your soul is ill—ill for love. The only thing that can cure you is Love, Love and more Love." Isadora and the doctor sensed a connection between them and began seeing each other. He was a very sensitive person, and being in his company began to restore her usual vigor and energy. Duncan became part of his life, accompanying him as he tended the war-wounded.

Still, she was puzzled about something. When Isadora had fallen ill, she had called him, but he had not come. Why, with his great kindness, passion, and love, had he stayed away? One night, she awoke and saw him. He had apparently been gazing at her while she lay sleeping. The look in his eyes was more than she could stand.

"Tell me what it is," she begged. "I can no longer bear this sinister mystery."

"Don't you know me?" he asked, his pleading eyes still fixed upon her.

She looked at him, as if for the first time, and memory flooded back. He was the doctor who had tried to save her children. With her recognition clear, he continued. "Now you know what I suffer. When you sleep, you look so like your little girl as she lay there. And I tried so hard to save her . . ."

The doctor and Isadora Duncan shared their tears that night and came to realize that they could not stay together and remain sane. They felt that a love based on such a tragic experience could never grow beyond it.

The tragic experience of war was also beginning to take its toll. Since England had immediately entered the war on France's side, hatred against Germany was great. Some of Isadora Duncan's pupils were still vacationing at Singer's English estate when the war began. Several of them were German. Staying in England could become uncomfortable for them. Singer arranged for the children to sail to neutral United States with Augustin Duncan. They stayed at a mansion in a suburb of New York City. Meanwhile, Elizabeth Duncan had moved her school from Darmstadt, Germany, to another New York suburb. Augustin and Elizabeth pleaded, by letter, for Isadora to join them in the United States and finally she agreed.

Duncan arrived in November 1914. She took a studio in New York City on Fourth Avenue and Twenty-third Street, which she named Dionysion. In early 1915, a group of friends arranged for Duncan to meet with the young mayor of New York, John Purroy Mitchell. His endorsement might help her gain financial support for her school, which she wished to relocate. Yet, at the gathering, Duncan insulted the women there, by making fun of their outfits, which she felt were pretentious. "Who are these women? Wives with feathers!" She then announced her support for Mrs. Ida Sniffen, who was in jail for killing her two illegitimate children.

Isadora Duncan and the Isadorables at the Booth Theater in
New York City in November 1914.

When Duncan was told that a mayor could not grant pardons,
she proceeded to lecture him on the poor education in the
United States as compared with the kind her pupils received.

Still, her work began again, and she flourished anew. Soon,
Isadora Duncan performed at the Metropolitan Opera House.
This engagement was very important to her. It was a test to see if
she could still dance in front of an audience. Duncan had to overcome the stage fright that had plagued her since her children's
deaths and the insecure times that followed. It was so easy for
Isadora Duncan to dance before Eleanora Duse, as she had done
during her recovery from her children's deaths. But Duncan worried about what she would do with thousands of people watching
her. She needn't have been so concerned. She still had the power
to fascinate and move an audience.

In December 1914, Duncan's six oldest pupils, known as the

Isadorables (Anna, Irma, Lisa, Theresa, Erica, and Margot), performed at Carnegie Hall in their American debut separate from Isadora Duncan. Reviews were good, and Duncan sent some of the money earned to the families of French children whose fathers were artists serving as soldiers in the war. A millionaire, Otto Kahn, made the Century Theater in New York City available to Duncan. For a month, she gave performances of dance with orchestral music and ancient Greek drama. Admission ranged from 10 cents to a dollar, but with those prices, there could be no profit, and empty seats guaranteed that no money would be made on this project.

Isadora Duncan had received a fine response artistically, but financially she could not survive. Jazz was in style. Duncan could not stomach what she considered the assault of this popular art, and she also criticized America's seemingly relaxed, uncaring attitude about the war going on in Europe. The United States was clearly against getting involved in the fighting, whereas Duncan passionately supported France.

Duncan's public pronouncements on these topics were unpopular but were in keeping with her ideas about society, which she viewed from outside the mainstream. Duncan's very unusual and difficult childhood and her many unhappy experiences had taught her the insecurity of life. Nevertheless, she was determined to live the way she thought was best, even if many people disapproved. She always felt she needed to defend, on principle, all that she did and believed. More and more, she railed not only against jazz but also against society in general. In doing so, she attacked the rich and powerful, on whom, of course, she depended for financial support. She became America's conscience, and like most persistent critics, she was considered a troublemaker. Certainly, she was a source of irritation. Usually Americans did not want to hear such criticisms.

That was not always the case, however. Near the end of a 1915 dance performance at the Metropolitan Opera House, Isadora Duncan gave one of her unrehearsed and critical speeches. She expressed her anger at rich Americans for not giving enough support to the arts. She declared that if she was ever to stay in the United States, these wealthy people should erect a theater on the

Lower East Side of New York, an area where thousands of the working poor lived, where people desperately wanted and would appreciate her dance.

Surprisingly, she received great applause, not only for her dance, but for her stinging lecture. Once she finished her final number, she returned 27 times for curtain calls.

But on the whole, public appeals for funds for her school failed, and Duncan decided to return to Europe. Once there, she traveled from country to country, living hand-to-mouth once more, trying to keep her school together and raise money for it. She feared wartime travel with her young pupils so she sent them temporarily to a Swiss boarding school (Switzerland was neutral in the war). She hoped eventually to set up a permanent school in Greece. Yet with the war lasting much longer than most people had predicted, Duncan's girls were no more than a moment away from its impact. She made desperate efforts to hang on, with the goal of returning to Bellevue at the war's end. To pay for the expenses of the children's Swiss boarding school, though, Duncan was forced to borrow money from lenders in Switzerland at an astonishing interest rate of 50 percent.

Duncan knew her bills had to be paid, but she promised to perform without pay at a war charity benefit in Paris in April 1916. It was there that she was truly idolized. She had received great emotional support in Paris after the death of her children, and her donation of time and talent in the war effort was deeply appreciated. She chose a wonderful set of dances for this performance, led by *La Marseillaise*, Rouget de Lisle's revolutionary anthem. Dressed in a bright red tunic, she rose from the ground, symbolizing the whole country. In the breathtaking finale, she defeated the enemy, and with breast bared, she stood before a wildly clapping audience.

Also in 1916, to help fulfill her financial obligations, she signed a contract to perform in South America. Off she sailed to Buenos Aires, Argentina, stopping briefly first in New York.

Soon after her arrival in Argentina, she and Augustin, who had joined her along the way, went to a students' cabaret. There, they got caught up in the passion of the tango and, upon being recognized, Duncan was begged to dance to their hymn for the

90

Isadora Duncan dances to *La Marseillaise*, France's revolutionary
national anthem, in 1915, during World War I.

freedom of Argentina. She did so, wrapping herself in the Argentinian national flag. Wild applause greeted her, and she returned to her hotel in high spirits.

However, her happiness lasted only one night. The next morning, her manager came to see her. He was furious at the reports of her performance, which he had read in the daily papers. Many Argentinians thought that her dancing to their national anthem while draped in their flag was a serious insult. Duncan's manager considered their contract broken, according to his understanding of the law. Subscriptions by the wealthiest families were being withdrawn, boycotts were threatened, and her Buenos Aires tour was ruined.

In addition to this bad news, a cable reached her from France that any money sent by her to support her school was being held up by war restrictions. The school was threatened with closing. With the vision of her girls being turned into the streets, she quickly sent Augustin with the money. But, she was left with none herself, so unplanned were her actions.

Yet she courageously went on with her South American tour. Montevideo in Uruguay and Rio de Janeiro in Brazil greeted Duncan's inspiring performances with enthusiasm. In Montevideo, she performed the stirring *Marseillaise* in front of a sold-out house, but she received only $300 for her efforts. When that money was shared with the theater and her agent, she was left with very little. Later concerts left her with similar small amounts of money. Thus, despite artistic success, she did not achieve her main goal: supporting her pupils.

Isadora Duncan returned to New York in September 1916. She was lonely and still greatly worried about the survival of the school.

Nevertheless, such worry never affected the integrity of her art and the ways in which she expressed it. Her faithfulness to her own philosophy of the dance remained strong. At one point, author Percy Mackaye had asked Duncan to give a tribute to his *Masque of Caliban* performance. Before going onstage, she was with a group of dancers trained by one of her imitators. When Duncan was spied, one of the dancers said to her, "If it weren't for you, we wouldn't be doing this. Don't you feel proud?"

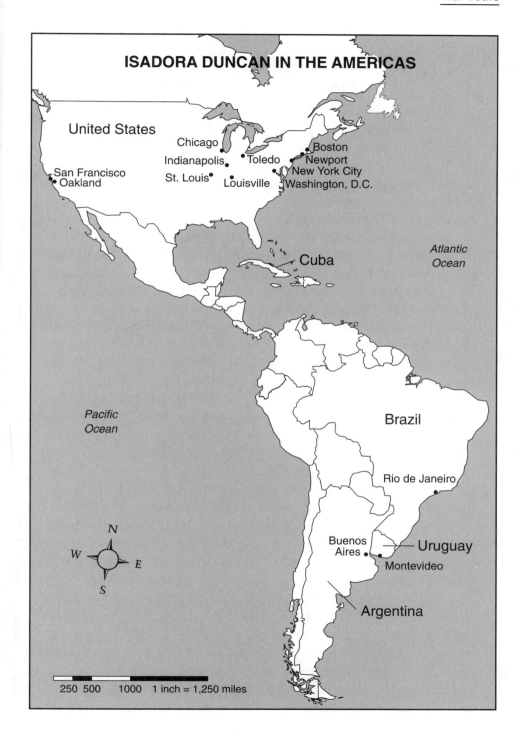

ISADORA DUNCAN IN THE AMERICAS

Duncan's response was almost startling. "I regard what you do with perfect horror."

Certainly the girl was crushed, but Isadora Duncan was speaking of a larger issue of dance—not the dancer's talent. "Their movements are all down," she explained later, "grovelling on the earth. They express nothing but the wisdom of the serpent, who crawls on his belly."

Isadora Duncan's dance technique always emphasized moving up. She danced to the heavens, to positive energy, and to reaching the stars. In her energy there was always the clear expression of freedom, ever upward.

By sheer coincidence, she came upon Paris Singer in New York. When he heard she was alone, with no money, he offered his customary rescue. He sent money to pay the children's boarding school bills. Duncan still loved him and was thrilled that he was with her, at least in some way, once more.

In November 1916, Singer set up a performance for her at the Metropolitan Opera House. On his own, he sent out invitations for it. Isadora Duncan described her moments on stage for this performance as one of the most beautiful times of her life.

Singer also cabled funds to Switzerland to bring the school to New York. The youngest of her students, however, had already been taken home by their parents. Duncan was pained by this disheartening news, but the arrival of Augustin and six of the older children cheered her.

Singer continued his generosity renting a studio for the group at Madison Square Garden, and they worked there every afternoon. His money and kindness had made life much easier for Duncan and her dancers. With a typical New York winter coming up, though, and Duncan not in very good health, Singer suggested a trip to Cuba.

After a winter in Cuba recuperating and regaining her dancing spirit, Duncan traveled to Palm Beach, Florida. Singer met her there, and he suggested a plan to locate her school permanently in Madison Square Garden, which he was in the process of buying. When Singer and Duncan returned to New York, he announced the plan publicly to their friends at a March 1917 dinner. Duncan insulted Singer by her reaction. She was very grateful, but it was still the middle of the war, and she was afraid of beginning such a huge project at that time. Also, she was obsessed with the idea of not being indebted to anyone, and this made it difficult for her to accept gifts graciously, especially such generous ones as this. Singer had years before proposed marriage to Isadora, but she had fallen in love with her pianist, Andre Capelet. Then she had flirted with another man when Singer offered to build a theater for her. When Singer had given her Bellevue, she loaned it to the French government. Now, she was being offered the princely gift of Madison Square Garden for her school. And instead of expressing appreciation, she held the plan up to public ridicule. Singer became so angered that he canceled his purchase of the Garden.

Regardless of the frustration Duncan caused Singer to feel, he had always returned to her. Isadora Duncan was quite different from anyone he had ever met in the wealthy circles of his life. She was, certainly, infuriating and unconventional. Her lack of a respectful attitude toward society was fascinating and upsetting to him. But she had goals and she was a person of action. Singer, though highly motivated, did not always follow through on his projects, but he was in awe of Duncan's total commitment to her goals. Her constant energy amazed him, especially since he never felt that he had to work.

Duncan had accepted gifts from him, but she always made sure that nothing made her feel inferior to him—or to anyone else. Her independence remained intact. This very independence eventually made him angrier than anything else. Yet, he had loved her basic kindness and gentleness, and sooner or later he was always drawn back to her.

At least until now, when Duncan finally insulted him in a way that he could not accept. She believed, as always, that he would return, but this was the beginning of the end of their relationship. His anger and hurt were too great, and he refused any attempt at reviving their long friendship. She lost the person who had been her savior countless times, Patrick's father, and a deeply loved friend.

The day after their argument, Isadora Duncan gave one of her most famous dance performances. On March 6, 1917, she danced at the Metropolitan Opera House and ended her performance with the French national anthem, *La Marseillaise*, and then *The Star-Spangled Banner*. At that point, she tore off her French revolutionary red tunic and revealed herself draped in an American flag. She was met with thunderous patriotic applause. Her dancing had been inspired by the Allies' bravery in the war. In addition, the United States was about ready to formally enter the war on the side of Britain and France. Duncan was further encouraged by the news of the growing opposition to the czar's oppressive rule in Russia. She danced with a spirit she had forgotten she possessed.

Duncan noted, "It is strange that in all my Art career it has been these movements of despair and revolt that have most attracted me. In my red tunic I have constantly danced the Revolution and the call to arms of the oppressed."

She danced with what she called "a fierce joy." It was a power that was both involving and frightening because it was so intense. It was from her soul, to please only her art. And clearly beyond even her control to restrain.

Duncan still felt deeply about leaving a legacy to her students, and the Isadorables were the only ones left. However, they had been voicing strong feelings about having greater artistic freedom from their teacher's control. The result was a growing rift, for she stated clearly that the young women weren't ready to perform alone. She needed them now, but they held firmly to their stand, and Duncan relented.

To help in case of immigration problems, she started proceedings to legally adopt them. They wouldn't have been able to enter the United States any other way, since the United States had declared war on Germany and some of the girls were therefore considered enemies. Three of the girls, Irma, Lisa, and Anna, adopted Isadora's last name permanently.

The Isadorables were renamed "The Isadora Duncan Dancers." From 1918 to 1920, they toured the United States in a series of concerts. They were hugely successful and left little doubt as to their ability to carry on the tradition set by Isadora Duncan. Their teacher finally saw it herself and accepted their readiness for complete independence. Duncan let them go, knowing that she had laid a solid foundation for their future careers.

On the other hand, she had one last hostile encounter with Singer. He became jealous of her dancing with a young man at a party he had given in her honor. She soon found herself penniless in New York without his financial support. Always creative, she sold gifts given her by Singer, such as an ermine coat and an emerald. She was then able to spend the summer with her girls, at Long Beach, Long Island. There, she saw her first movie.

At first, she refused to go inside the movie theater. But she was too curious not to. Once the film was over, she admitted it had been fun. Later in life, Duncan was offered movie deals, but she never accepted. She believed the jumpy frames of the movie would make her dance seem like a nervous condition. It was not one of the memories she wished to leave to the ages.

As was Duncan's habit, she spent the money she had without a practical plan, so when summer ended, she was broke again. To

Dancers in Kentucky. After World War I, the Isadora Duncan Dancers toured the United States without Isadora Duncan.

earn money, she accepted a contract to dance in California. It had been 22 years since she had left San Francisco, and the return was an emotional one.

San Francisco in 1917, was altogether new to her, changed greatly after the disastrous earthquake and fire of 1906. Changed, as well, was her mother. Because of homesickness, Dora Duncan had refused to stay in Europe. Duncan had not seen her in years. To Isadora's eyes, "she looked very old and careworn and once, lunching out at the Cliff House [a restaurant high on cliffs overlooking the Pacific Ocean], and seeing our two selves in a mirror, I could not help contrasting my sad face and the haggard looks of my mother with the two adventuresome spirits who had set out twenty-two years ago with such high hopes to seek fame and fortune. Both had been found—why was the result so tragic?"

She wondered whether happiness ever really existed over an extended period of time. She felt, perhaps, "there were only moments."

Isadora Duncan gives a charity performance to raise money to help the European victims of World War I.

If that was true, she had some of those happy "moments" during her work with pianist Harold Bauer, whom she met in San Francisco. Bauer, upon meeting her, explained the effect Duncan had had on his life. He had seen her years before, dancing in Paris. At that time, he had been having trouble with his musical technique on the piano. In watching her, however, he had found a solution to his problem. Seeing her rhythmic movements, an idea about how to use loud and soft tones creatively came to him. He thus had great respect for Duncan's art, and that feeling was mutual. Her performance, accompanied by Bauer, at the Columbia Theater was a true highlight of this period and, indeed, of her life.

Yet, given the brief nature of moments, Duncan's happiness did not last. There was little support in the city of her birth for a future school of dance, and that deeply saddened her. There were already other schools, imitators as she saw them, and they were well established. But none of them, in her view, was able to communicate the vision of America she had always felt could be expressed through dance.

She still saw jazz as a primary villain. "It seems to me," she explained, "monstrous that any one should believe that the Jazz rhythm expresses America. . . . America's music would be something different. It has yet to be written . . . some day it will gush forth from the great stretches of Earth, rain down from the vast sky spaces, and America will be expressed in some Titanic music that will shape its chaos to harmony. . . .

She believed ballet and jazz to be mutant forms of dance, somehow unclean. She even felt American women were not built to dance ballet because of their long legs and free spirit. "Let them," she declared, "come forth with great strides, leaps and bounds, with lifted forehead and far-spread arms. . . . That will be America dancing."

CHAPTER ELEVEN

Revolutionary Dancer

The years that made up most of Isadora Duncan's last decade of life were a whirlwind of passionate activity, both artistically and personally. More than ever, Duncan confronted a changed world, one often hostile to her and her art.

World War I had ended in 1918 with the victory of the Allies and the defeat of Germany. During the last year of the war, Bolsheviks (Communists) had seized power in Russia. Economic dislocations caused by the ending of the war resulted in high unemployment and workers' strikes in the United States. In 1919, race riots occurred across the country. That explosion of bigotry was joined by governmental and public reaction against the Russian Revolution. Some people feared that racial and labor problems were omens of a coming revolution in the United States. For a brief period in 1919 and the early 1920s, the United States underwent the so-called Red Scare. Red was the favored color for the flags and banners of revolutionaries and radicals. Communists were called Reds. Political radicals were accused of threatening to overthrow the government, and hundreds were forced to leave the country. Immigrants, supposedly having radical foreign ideas, were persecuted.

During the 1920s, the economy improved, but these reactionary attitudes lingered on. Despite the nation's apparent economic health, many of the rich grew richer while the incomes of the poor did not increase much if at all. Warren G. Harding probably best expressed the attitudes of many Americans during his successful campaign for U.S. President in 1920:

America's present need is not heroics, but healing; not nostrums, but normalcy; not revolution, but restoration; not agitation, but adjustment; not surgery, but serenity; not the dramatic, but the dispassionate;

not experiment, but equipoise; not submergence in internationality, but sustainment in triumphant nationality.

This popularly held ideal of American life was, of course, in direct opposition to the heroic, revolutionary, dramatic, experimental dance of Isadora Duncan, who wished to express what she claimed was her uniquely American dance in the United States. But if her own country viewed her as a troublemaker and wouldn't support her dance movement, she would continue to search for help on the international scene.

A few years after the war, Isadora Duncan revisited Greece, with five of the six former students who were now known as the Isadora Duncan Dancers. The group was accompanied by the great American photographer Edward Steichen. At the Parthenon in Athens, he took some of the most famous photographs of Isadora Duncan. The goal of her trip was to revive the Greek government's interest in setting up a school of dance in Athens, but she failed. Nevertheless, she did see how far her former pupils, now young women, had come. Their views on dance had grown greatly, and they now offered their thoughts on musical interpretation. It was a source of pride for the great teacher. Nevertheless, Anna, one of the remaining five, eventually left the group. She had become involved in a romantic relationship with Walter Rummel, their accompanist. The separation was necessary because Rummel was also involved with Isadora Duncan herself.

From Greece, Duncan returned to France. She danced at the Theatre des Champs-Elysees in Paris and toured Belgium, the Netherlands, and England. Word had gone out that Duncan was leaving for Communist-controlled Russia, where she had an offer from the government for a school of dance in Moscow. The reaction to her going to Russia was quite mixed. Her popularity as a dancer was in her favor, but anger about her support of Communist ideas was not. Because of this, some of her European performances were conducted in half-empty theaters. However, her concert in London was an affecting, emotional one, and at the end there was much appreciation.

She tried not to leave for Russia until she could see her mother, who was traveling by ship to London from the United States. Because Dora Duncan's arrival was greatly delayed, Isadora left before they could meet. Isadora did bid a tearful good-bye to two former Isadorables, Lisa and Theresa, who refused to go to Russia. Duncan had once labeled these young dancers ungrateful, but now she held them in deep affection.

When Duncan went to Russia, only Irma came. Lisa and Margot were in France. Anna, Theresa, and Erica eventually went to the United States. Yet, despite the dancers' separation from their great teacher, they proudly used their lives and talents to express her innovative ideas and upheld her high standards.

"On the way to Russia," Duncan later remarked, looking back, "I had the detached feeling of a soul after death making its way to another sphere. I thought I had left all forms of European life behind me forever. I actually believed that the ideal state, such as Plato, Karl Marx, and Lenin had dreamed it, had now by some miracle been created on earth. With all the energy of my being, disappointed in the attempts to realize any of my art visions in

Irma Duncan with students at the Moscow dance school in the Soviet Union, which opened in 1921.

Europe, I was ready to enter the ideal domain of Communism."

Her school opened in 1921 with a major performance at the Bolshoi Theater, which was filled to its capacity of 3,000. Barriers had to be removed to accommodate the overflow crowd. Once Vladimir Lenin, head of the Soviet government and Communist Party, had arrived, the performance began. Duncan performed the *Marche Slav*, a dance of depth and feeling. The music was by Tchaikovsky. The *Marche Slav* dealt with a slave in chains (symbolizing Russia before the Communist Revolution in 1917), fighting for his freedom, breaking the bonds, and emerging victorious. The audience was greatly moved. The finale, with Irma Duncan leading a stage full of children dressed in red tunics, brought the audience to its feet. Even Lenin was standing and singing the *Internationale*, the Communist anthem, with the rest.

Isadora Duncan was moved as never before, especially by Lenin's reaction and his loud voice crying, "Bravo!"

Personal love bloomed anew when she met the famous Russian poet Sergey Esenin, who was 18 years younger than she.

Isadora Duncan and Russian poet Sergey Esenin were married right before their tours of Europe and the United States.

They were married five months later, in May 1922. The couple traveled to Germany, Belgium, France, and Italy before sailing to the United States where Duncan had arranged for a dance tour. She wanted to earn money for the Moscow school. Once in New York City, they were detained at Ellis Island as Soviet citizens. At that time the United States did not diplomatically recognize Communist-controlled Russia. The famous couple was held for interrogation.

Esenin had offered a written statement explaining that he and Duncan weren't politicians. They were only artists. He declared in his statement that understanding between people of the two countries was very important.

Immigration officials wanted to find out whether either of them carried any anti-American literature with them. They wanted to seize any propaganda that might advocate overthrowing the United States government or that might spread Communist ideas. Every single piece of their belongings was searched, including Esenin's poems and Duncan's musical scores.

Finally, after being held until the next day, they were released and allowed to leave Ellis Island for Manhattan across New York Harbor. Though technically innocent, Duncan always felt she and Esenin were made to feel guilty. Later, this incident led to her being called "Red" in the United States, and the accusation followed her for the rest of her life.

Yet, cheering audiences greeted her at Carnegie Hall in October 1922, for she was at the very top of her form. She danced to life, to eternity, and to nature's long-lasting love for children. Yet, Duncan's response, at intermission, was, "Now I have finished. I have said all I have to say tonight. But because the manager insists upon variety, I must go on and do the *Seventh Symphony*, and I have no heart for it. I should stop now."

Still, there was a moment of almost unspeakable beauty, when, at a studio luncheon, Isadora Duncan and the great Russian dancer and choreographer Nijinsky danced together. She created the dance spontaneously and Nijinsky followed as if they had been partners for years and as if the dance had been fully choreographed. Nijinsky, with his great talent, was meshing perfectly with what Duncan was creating at that very moment.

However, fiery political speeches by Duncan in Boston brought bad publicity. At the time, red was considered evil, and terror greeted anything related to Russia and communism. But Isadora Duncan never minced her words, and because of these speeches, her concert dates were canceled.

After asking for school financing from the United States, Duncan said, "America has all that Russia has not! Russia has things that America has not! Why will America not reach out a hand to Russia, as I have given my hand?"

She continued her crusade, and in the midst of an emotional

Duncan and Esenin aroused controversy during their travels in the United States.

speech about the art of the human body, she added, as she held a red scarf over her head, "This is red! So am I! It is the color of life and vigor. . . . You don't know what beauty is!"

Boston's mayor soon banned Duncan from appearing there, in order to protect "the decent element." Investigations into the possibility of deporting her began in the departments of Labor, Justice, and State when they were informed that the red sash Duncan raised over her head rendered her nude in public. In response, Isadora Duncan was typically controversial: "Why should I care what part of my body I reveal? Why is one part more evil than another? . . . I don't know why this Puritan vulgarity should be confined to Boston, but it seems to be. Other cities are not afflicted with a horror of beauty and a smirking taste for burlesque semi-exposures."

She traveled to Indianapolis where four detectives waited backstage to make sure she would stay clothed. In Louisville, Kentucky, where just a shoulder strap broke, she made headlines. Her red costumes were confiscated by the mayor's order in another city, which kept Duncan from doing some of her revolutionary dances. To this insult, Duncan responded on stage, claiming that the mayor had stolen them because of his love of red things. On her departure to France from New York, in January 1923, she waved a red flag from the boat. Duncan's reason? "I waved the flag only to make them mad."

Yet, despite this act of defiance, Isadora Duncan tried to set things straight. "I am not an anarchist or Bolshevist. My husband and I are revolutionists. All geniuses worthy of the name are . . . Goodbye America. I shall never see you again."

Duncan's health, always a concern, worsened again. Esenin's behavior, owing greatly to his problems with alcohol, turned disturbing and violent.

At the start of 1923, Isadora Duncan left for France, with Esenin. At midyear she performed twice at the Trocadéro and then went on to Moscow. Once there, she separated from her husband, and rested for most of the remaining part of the year.

There was a rebirth, of sorts, for Isadora Duncan. Upon the death of Lenin in 1924, she composed two funeral marches and performed them to overwhelming praise. She continued to develop the revolutionary direction of her work, begun with the *Marseillaise* and the *Marche Slav. Dubinushka, The Warshavianka,* and *The Blacksmith* were the results. These dances made use of work movements, such as hauling ropes or hammering. They gained wide publicity, even in the United States where the great dancer Martha Graham performed *The Revolt* with dancing influenced by Duncan.

Duncan toured what was then called the Soviet Union (Russia and surrounding Communist lands) through September, until her final performance at the Bolshoi in Moscow. Duncan's reception was perhaps the most memorable and emotionally satisfying of her career.

Duncan left Russia forever and arrived in Berlin in September 1924. She was anxious to raise needed funds for her school in the Soviet Union. However, because she had not been in Berlin eight days before the performance was scheduled, the manager with whom she had signed the contract charged that she had broken it and would not pay her. Isadora was left deserted, and no one in her family was able to or felt compelled to help. Eventually, Augustin sent whatever he could afford. She seemed to feel closest to him and was deeply grateful for all he did. Yet, it wasn't nearly enough. Her house in Neuilly was about to be seized, and even with last-minute help from a close friend from the wartime years, Duncan still spent money irresponsibly. When her credit was cut off in some restaurants, she ate elsewhere. Eventually, it all caught up to her when her original students were dispersed, the Moscow school was barely alive, and Irma Duncan and the Russian school made a tour of China without telling her. Isadora and Irma were eventually reconciled when Isadora's mother died and they met in Germany. They parted as friends, and the Moscow school managed to go on for many years.

Still, Duncan remained unhappy with her lack of money and career opportunities in Germany. With the help of an American newspaper reporter, who became a good friend, she settled her Berlin debts and returned to Paris at the end of 1924.

Another personal grim period arose when Margot, an Isadorable, died of influenza early in 1925. Margot's death came as a deep sadness and reawakened the horror of Isadora's own children's deaths, 12 years before. She wrote about this to Irma Duncan: "Nobody realized it, but poor little Margot's death was the finishing touch. I simply almost gave up entirely. I am just recovering from the ghastly cruelty and terror of the whole thing. I confess—I can't understand—the whole scheme of things is too unbearable."

Adding to her sadness was the fact that she was not able to be with her Russian pupils, and most tragically, Esenin committed suicide in Leningrad at the year's end. Esenin had complained of boredom and lack of purpose. He could never feel fulfilled again and believed he had nothing more to give. He wrote a short poem in his own blood on the day he died because the hotel, he explained, had no ink. The poem was his farewell to a friend, who was also a poet. The poem also expressed his disillusionment with the Communist dictatorship, which he said no longer needed him or his poems.

The newspapers in France and the United States fed hungrily on this news and published many stories about Isadora Duncan's life with Esenin. She was furious and cabled her anger to news agencies: "The news of the tragic death of Esenin has caused me the deepest pain. He had youth, beauty, genius. Not content with these gifts, his audacious spirit sought the unattainable, and he wished to lay low the Philistines.

"He had destroyed his young and splendid body, but his soul will live eternally in the soul of the Russian people and in the souls of those who love the poets. I protest strongly against the frivolous and inexact statements printed in the American press in Paris. There was never between Esenin and myself any quarrel or divorce. I weep over his death with anguish and despair."

Duncan's financial stress continued. Despite some new performances with Russian pianist Victor Seroff in 1926, she was forced, near the end of the year, to begin writing her autobiography. She hoped the book would earn enough to ease her money problems. She only worked on it from time to time, but she meant to fulfill her contractual obligations.

Seroff had befriended her at an important time. It was more than their love of music that brought them together. Seroff, whom Duncan called Vitya, was one of the few people with whom she could talk about her time in Russia. He had been there during the Russian Revolution in 1917 and both shared the aftermath. He admired Esenin. To Seroff, Esenin was more than a troublemaker— he was an artist. Seroff was also close to Esenin's age and understood what life with Isadora Duncan was like. Duncan was able to talk with him about the most private things, especially about Esenin. Seroff also teased her, joked with her, and cheered her up. Now, with her growing money problems, she needed all the joy possible.

Her career was almost at a standstill. She was no longer

young or in fashion. Her appeal was limited on that level and her politics seemed too extreme for many. She might have gained some of her audience back if she spoke believably about communism's failings, but her school was in Russia, so she couldn't risk that government's anger.

Duncan's work lacked its previous verve and imagination. She just didn't have the passion left within her to put into her performances or her school. Esenin's death troubled her deeply and she was, despite Seroff's friendship, still haunted by her children's deaths. She found it very difficult to be around young children, and her friends kept their children away as much as possible.

During the last year of her life, she lived part of the time on the French Riviera and part of the time in Paris Her final performance came in July 1927 at the Mogador Theater in that city. She had been rehearsing and dieting with great intensity for this first performance in front of a large audience in several years. Duncan seemed to know this was her finale and performed only her most serious work. By the time she was done, the audience, quiet throughout, exploded in applause and tears.

Isadora Duncan and Mary Desti left the French capital on a trip south to the Riviera and arrived in Nice, deep in debt. Victor Seroff joined them, only to decide to leave for Paris to try to raise money for Duncan. She even asked Desti to see Paris Singer, who was staying in a resort town nearby. Despite showing kindness and concern, according to Mary Desti, he refused to help because he believed the money would just be misspent. Duncan occupied much of her time in search of a man she had seen in a café who drove off in a Bugatti racing car. She had seen the expensive car on the road previously and said she wanted to ride in it.

Upon finding the driver, and believing jealousy would make Singer wish he were back with her, she seemed thrilled. Duncan set out to execute her plan with her usual singlemindedness and spontaneity.

CHAPTER TWELVE

The End and the Beginning

Many people have wondered about Isadora Duncan's state of mind as summer became fall in 1927. Her dear friend Mary Desti wrote of her as a woman who had largely given up on life. Victor Seroff, who had been close to Duncan for some time, later showed a September 14 letter, written by her to him, and asserted that she had offered "no word of self-pity but calm despair and gentle sorrow."

Whatever her mood, and Duncan changed hers often, the events near Paris are clear. After a dinner on the evening of September 14 with Mary Desti, Isadora Duncan was about to go off for a drive with Benoit Falchetto, an agent for the Bugatti sports car company. He was the man she had seen earlier. She was wearing her well-used red woolen shawl. It was an especially raw night for early fall, but Duncan felt fine. Even with Desti's warnings, because Desti felt uneasy with her friend's excitement, Duncan simply replied, "My dear, I would go for this ride tonight even if I were sure it would be my last. Even then, I would go quicker."

The ride that followed, tragically, was exactly that—her last.

Mary Desti saw the car pull away slowly, and before it had gone far, she noticed the shawl dangling out of the closed door. The car stopped suddenly, and Mary went running toward it. She found Isadora seated, in the seat on the passenger's side, just as she had been when she left. Her head was facing down, held taut by the shawl against the side of the car.

The Bugatti was a racing car, which was built very low to the ground. The car had no mudguards, flaps made to protect the wheels from damage by dirt. Duncan had thrown her long shawl over her shoulder, the fringe caught the rear wheel by her left side. As the wheel turned, the scarf tightened around her neck, breaking it and killing her instantly.

She was taken by her brother Raymond, Mary Desti, and Victor Seroff to be buried in Paris. Before the flower-covered coffin was put in the hearse, Raymond Duncan draped it with an American flag. Mary Desti rearranged ribbons of scarlet gladioli, so the gold-imprinted phrase "The Heart of Russia Weeps for Isadora" was clearly seen.

At the cemetery, perhaps as many as 10,000 people gathered. Police were unable to hold the crowds back. People who had seen her dance decades before came to pay their respects. Tears of

Elizabeth, Augustin, and Raymond Duncan after the funeral of their sister, Isadora, in 1927.

students flowed freely. Soldiers marked the importance of the occasion with a solemn bowing of their heads.

Her body was cremated, and her ashes put next to her children's in the memorial created for them. It would have made Duncan happy to have watched the scene of working people, shopkeepers, and street vendors all stopping their labors to watch the funeral service. Children were lifted on shoulders to see the great dancer moving on. She would surely have understood this outpouring. It was the masses, these hard workers, who needed freedom so desperately, and the children, who knew so much about it naturally, who mattered most to her. There was always a childlike quality in Isadora Duncan that remained a part of her when she grew up to be the adult who became so famous.

Isadora Duncan was a wonderfully special mix of style and action. She was a person who has had a permanent effect on the art of dance, and she succeeded in liberating people in ways no one had known before. She understood what made people feel free and how freedom affected their lives.

Perhaps the part of her legacy that defines Isadora Duncan most clearly is the creation of schools of dance for young children. Young people can be molded and are always open to new feelings and experiences. It never mattered to Duncan that not every child would dance professionally or even be talented enough to do so. The deep feeling for natural rhythms and movements would have been instilled in them.

Appreciation of the value of Duncan's legacy for future generations was a long time coming. It was not until the 1970s, almost half a century after her death, that American dance acknowledged the philosophy and work of Isadora Duncan as one of its foundations. As she so deeply wished, she had laid the building blocks of the "Dance of America," expressed with complete freedom of spirit. She captured in dance what Walt Whitman, the poet she so much admired, expressed in his poems, such as "Song of the Open Road" and "I See America Singing." She often felt spiritually connected to him, and he was the inspiration for some of Duncan's most deeply meaningful and enduring work.

Isadora Duncan's legacy is also international. A school of dance in central Europe uses her theories of natural movement.

Japan held an Isadora Duncan Festival in 1991. An Isadora Duncan Foundation thrives in New York City. She is a constant source of inspirational ideas and study. In a world filled with daily, sometimes powerful pressure to be like everybody else, Isadora Duncan's dance sets us free.

Yet, for all the international influence Isadora Duncan has had, her most lasting value may be seen in the eyes of a dancing child as they glisten with the pure thrill of natural movement. "To her, it is a joy to dance; to me it is a joy to watch her," Duncan once said as she observed one of her students.

Her ideas about how to teach dance to children were fundamentally different from any that had been put into practice before: "The child must not be taught to make movements, but

Children in Potsdam, Germany, at a commemoration of the dance of Isadora Duncan, soon after her tragic death.

her soul, as it grows to maturity must be guided and instructed; in other words, the body must be taught to express itself by means of the motions which are natural to it."

Duncan always believed that true art was achieved over a lifetime filled with devotion and commitment. She felt that knowledge of the full meaning of dance begins with training the body before the age of nine. This was why she taught young children. Teaching was part of her own life's commitment, and she never charged for her dancing instruction. It was a way of offering her legacy of imagination and beauty.

She believed deeply that any big change in the art of dancing would not be led by a teacher, but rather would come from the energy and innocence of children. In all her efforts, sometimes successful and sometimes not, to keep her schools going, it was always to use movements as a way to reach grace in living.

Isadora Duncan lived the way she pleased and ignored many of society's rules. There was nothing false in her manner. She was who she was. Life was too important not to be honest. Her dance, like her life, was generated by ideas that seemed to flash into her mind on the spur of the moment. If things felt right, she did them, yet they were never carelessly expressed. Thus, her choreography appeared spontaneous but most of it was not. Her friend Rodin, the great French sculptor, was delighted with the product of this union of pure inspiration and careful expression. He called it "feeling without effort, that was and is so completely fascinating. The feeling is there and gone, but never forgotten."

She had the unique ability through dance to make life clearer for those who saw her. Just as the Greek philosopher Socrates, whom she greatly admired, used a system of questioning to reveal a deeper truth to his students, so Isadora Duncan danced to offer a deeper understanding of life. Therefore, learning was a function of living and dance could not be a skill separated from it. Duncan's teaching was not only movement generated, but part of a larger whole which included a gesture, a glance, a word of encouragement. They were all designed to create feeling rather than force routine. She stated plainly, "Why should not the rapture which touches children into ineffable beauty be the birthright of every child in the land?"

Isadora Duncan must be regarded as one of the few artists of great and lasting power who used their magic not only to create enjoyment, praise, or applause in theaters but also to change our world.

The change is certainly most clear in the art of the dance, for which her work was a magnificent expression of the way in which music and body can be used together. She applied her great intelligence effectively because she kept things simple. Though her dances had few movements, they said more than the most complicated, rigidly arranged movements. To express deep feeling simply is a great challenge, and she met this challenge splendidly.

Yet, she did more, because she influenced our social and moral lives. She demonstrated the beauty of freedom. She created an atmosphere where girls and boys could look upon natural grace with a lack of fear. She encouraged escape from the conformity and repeated tasks that often crush individual expression.

Through her use and appreciation of the art and philosophy of ancient Greece, she demonstrated how the past might show the way to a future where humankind could move in harmony with nature. She is, by these accomplishments, as much a part of history as any leader or conqueror who occupies the pages of textbooks.

Life may have often frustrated and saddened Isadora Duncan, but it could never contain her. She lived for the moment, and practical matters held little interest for her. She was irresponsible with money, often spending what she didn't have and hoping someone else would clear up her financial problems. Love seemed to consist of a series of temporary states rather than a commitment to one other person. Duncan had affairs with many men and gave birth to three illegitimate children. While the United States remained neutral during the first years of World War I, Isadora Duncan was passionately pro-France and so pro-war. In accordance with her own revolutionary temperament, when the Red Scare hit after the Russian Revolution, Duncan waved the color red like a banner. Her praise of Russia and criticism of the United States provoked angry controversy and made her unpopular in many quarters.

Communist Russia, in the first years after the Revolution in

This photograph of Isadora Duncan at the Parthenon was taken by the noted photographer Edward Steichen in 1920.

1917, was still chaotic, without order, and unsure of its direction. However, it was the only nation that didn't turn away from Duncan's desire for a school supported by the government. Nevertheless, she was, with all her apparent anti-U.S. feeling, first and foremost, American.

The United States in the early 20th century had been a melting pot. Isadora Duncan rarely shied away from that kind of disorder, where freedom runs in many directions, especially when it involved upsetting the routine through deeply felt action. When she criticized the United States, she was exercising the right to speak that is so completely American. In a 1922 Boston speech, she displayed anger at the lack of American appreciation of art and real freedom. Although citizens in Boston would not accept her ideas, neither would she ignore things she believed were wrong. Most people in the United States, however, were not yet ready for her wisdom, nor mature enough for her vision. What she said was actually consistent with democratic American traditions of searching for big answers and positive change. Freedom is always at the heart of what the United States wants to stand for, and Duncan felt she was only using her freedom as it was meant to be used. That she felt forced to leave the country did not, in her heart, make her any less a part of it.

Isadora Duncan understood that her dreams had to be rooted in the possibility of their becoming real. If what she believed could happen was right, then her dreams were also possible. But her impatience, along with rash decisions, often betrayed her, especially since she wouldn't play anyone's game and hated bureaucracy. What she knew was right and true was not easily accepted in the everyday life of the time, but she never stopped trying.

Her triumph lies in the fact that her vision remains very much alive. Many movements created and executed by famous dance companies, choreographers, and dancers today are based on her approach to dance. Those who had the honor to see Isadora Duncan perform were privileged. Those who see children today, flying across a theater stage in airy costumes to the music of the wind, are different because she danced.

1877   May 26, Angela Isadora Duncan is born in San Francisco, the youngest of four children.

1892   Isadora teaches social dancing in the Oakland area with her sister Elizabeth.

1895   Duncan travels with her mother to Chicago and begins work at the Masonic Temple Roof Garden. She becomes part of Augustin Daly's theater group and comes to New York.

1898   Duncan performs at Carnegie Hall to the music of Ethelbert Woodbridge Nevin.

1899   Duncan leaves for London with her family.

1900   Duncan gives recitals under Charles Hallé's direction at the New Gallery, London. She joins her brother Raymond in Paris and visits the Louvre.

1901   Duncan performs in private homes. She forms friendships with painter Eugène Carrière and singer Mary Desti.

1902   Duncan joins Loie Fuller's company and debuts in Vienna, Austria.

1903   Duncan performs in Berlin, Germany, and has her official Paris debut performance. The Duncan family goes to Athens, Greece, where the study of Greek culture influences her dance philosophy and style.

1904   At the Bayreuth Festival in Germany, Duncan appears in *Tannhäuser*, where her costuming causes controversy. She falls in love with Edward Gordon Craig.

1905   Duncan begins a tour of Russia. She starts to understand the poverty of the masses. Duncan begins a school of dance in Grünewald, Germany, and gives birth to daughter, Deirdre. She and Craig work with Eleanora Duse on Ibsen's play *Rosmersholm*.

1908   Duncan dances at the Metropolitan Opera House, directed by Walter Damrosch. She tours the United States and is praised by President Theodore Roosevelt.

1909   Duncan meets Paris Singer, who backs a school of dance for her.

1910   Patrick, son of Duncan and Singer, is born in France.

1913   Deirdre and Patrick die accidentally by drowning in the Seine River. Duncan visits Albania to help starving children.

1914   Singer gives Duncan a new school of dance at Bellevue called Dionysion. A son is born and dies a few hours after birth. Duncan gives Dionysion to the French government for the war effort. She goes to New York and performs at the Metropolitan.

1917   Duncan files to legally adopt her dancers, the Isadorables. She visits San Francisco.

1921   Duncan opens a dance school in Moscow.

1922   Duncan marries Russian poet Sergey Esenin. She is detained with him at Ellis Island in New York Harbor on suspicion of being a Communist sympathizer. She delivers a fiery political speech in Boston, which causes concerts to be canceled.

1923   Duncan leaves the United States forever.

1925   Esenin commits suicide.

1926   Duncan, penniless, begins her autobiography.

1927   Duncan returns to Paris, where she dies accidentally of strangulation in a car accident.

anarchist A person who believes in or advocates the political ideal that all governments are unnecessary and undesirable; according to anarchists, people should abolish governments and work together voluntarily to meet their own and society's needs. Some anarchists advocate the overthrow of organized government by force.

bankruptcy The legal process by which a person or company that cannot pay its debts has a court decide how the person's or company's financial matters should be run to pay off the money owed or how the remaining property should be distributed among those to whom money is owed. Once the process is complete, the person or company is legally free of past debts.

choreography The art of creating, composing, and arranging dances.

communism A system of political and economic beliefs based on the ideas of Marx and Lenin. In theory, private property is eliminated, people own and control the means of production in common, economic goods and services are distributed fairly, and the state plays a minimum role in people's lives. In reality, in the Soviet Union and elsewhere, a single dictatorial Communist Party controlled the government, the economy, and the means of production.

curtain call A performer's appearance requested by audience applause after the end of a play or other performance.

debut A first public appearance or performance.

deportation The removal or sending back of an alien (a foreign-born or other person who has not qualified as a citizen) to the country from which he or she came because that person's presence is considered unlawful or inconsistent with public welfare.

encore A demand made by an audience for the repetition of part of a performance or for an additional performance. Sometimes the word refers to the actual reappearance or additional performance given in response to such a demand.

lyrics The words of a song.

pantomime A dramatic or dancing performance in which a story is told by one or more performers' bodily and facial movements rather than through dialogue.

toga A loose white woolen outer garment made of a single piece of cloth draped gracefully around the body and worn in public by male citizens of ancient Rome and by young Roman boys and girls whose garments had a purple stripe.

troupe A group or company of dancers or theatrical performers.

tunic A simple shirt usually made with short sleeves and usually knee length or longer, belted at the waist, and worn as an under or outer garment by men and women in ancient Greece and Rome.

tutu A short skirt often worn by ballerinas during classical ballet performances.

BIBLIOGRAPHY

AND RECOMMENDED READINGS

Blair, Fredericka. *Isadora: Portrait of the Artist as a Woman*. New York: McGraw-Hill, 1986.

Cheney, Sheldon, ed. *The Art of the Dance*. New York: Theatre Arts Books, 1928, 1969.

Craig, Edward G. *Index to the Story of My Days*. New York: Viking Press, 1957.

Croce, Arlene. *After Images*. New York: Alfred Knopf, 1978.

———. *Sight Lines*. New York: Alfred Knopf, 1987.

Desti, Mary. *The Untold Story—The Life of Isadora Duncan, 1921-27*. New York: Liveright Press, 1929; New York: Da Capo Press, 1981.

Duncan, Irma. *Isadora Duncan: Pioneer in the Art of Dance*. New York: New York Public Library, 1958.

Duncan, Isadora. *My Life*. New York: Liveright Publishing Company, 1927.

Loewenthal, Lillian. *The Search for Isadora*. Pennington, New Jersey: Princeton Book Company, 1993.

McVay, Gordon. *Isadora and Esenin*. Ann Arbor, Michigan: Ardis Press, 1980.

Nietzsche, Frederic. *The Birth of Tragedy*. New York: Doubleday, 1956.

Rosemont, Franklin, ed. *Isadora Speaks*. San Francisco: City Lights, 1981.

Schneider, Ilya Ilyitch. *Isadora Duncan: The Russian Years*. London: Macdonald Publishing, 1968.

Seroff, Victor. *The Real Isadora*. New York: Dial Press, 1971.

Steegmuller, Francis. *Your Isadora*. New York: Random House, 1974.

Miami Beach, Florida	• Dance Arts Foundation, Inc., 1531 West 22 Street, offers performances of the Isadora Duncan Dance Ensemble.
New York City	• DanceArt Isadora, Inc.; 75 East End Avenue. This group has a performing company, the Duncan Dance Continuum, and offers classes, and workshops.
	• Isadora Duncan Foundation for Contemporary Dance, Inc.; 141 West 26 Street. This organization has a resident performing company, Lori Belilove & Company, and offers classes, workshops, and teacher training. It also has videos, films, and photos.
	• Isadora Duncan International Institute, Inc., is affiliated with New York University and the Dance Center of the 92nd Street Y. It offers classes, performances, workshops and study abroad.
Paris, France	• Théâtre des Champs-Elysées. Sculptures by Emile-Antoine Bourdelle on the outside of the building depict Isadora Duncan in several scenes. Inside, four murals painted by Maurice Denis show women based on Duncan's image.

ACKNOWLEDGMENTS

The author acknowledges with gratitude the following sources:

Blair, Fredericka, *Isadora: Portrait of the Artist as a Woman*, New York: McGraw-Hill, 1986; Cheney, Sheldon, ed., *The Art of the Dance*, New York: Theatre Arts Books, 1928, 1969; Craig, Edward G., *Index to the Story of My Days*, New York: Viking, 1957; Croce, Arlene, *After Images*, New York: Alfred Knopf, 1987; Desti, Mary, *The Untold Story—The Life of Isadora Duncan, 1921–27*, New York: Liveright Press, 1929, and Da Capo Press, 1981; Duncan, Irma, *Isadora Duncan: Pioneer in the Art of Dance*, New York: New York Public Library, 1958; Duncan, Isadora, *My Life*, New York: Liveright Publishing Corporation, 1927, 1955; Loewenthal, Lillian, *The Search for Isadora*, Pennington, New Jersey: Princeton Book Company, 1993; McVay, Gordon, *Isadora and Esenin*, Ann Arbor, Michigan: Ardis Press, 1980; Nietzsche, Frederic, *The Birth of Tragedy*, New York: Doubleday, 1956; Rosemont, Franklin, ed., *Isadora Speaks*, San Francisco: City Lights, 1981; Schneider, Ilya Ilyiytch, *Isadora Duncan: The Russian Years*, London: Macdonald Publishing, 1968; Seroff, Victor, *The Real Isadora*, New York: Dial Press, 1971; Steegmuller, Francis, *Your Isadora*, New York: Random House, 1974.

Larry Sandomir has been an educator since 1972. He has taught in public and private schools in New York City in grades 5 through 8. He also works as an editor for a writing school and has been named twice in *The Who's Who of Teaching in America*. Sandomir is married to the finest teacher he knows and has three children. He resides in Manhattan.

James P. Shenton is Professor of History at Columbia University. He has taught American History since 1951. Among his publications are *Robert John Walker, a Politician from Jackson to Lincoln; An Historian's History of the United States*; and *The Melting Pot*. Professor Shenton is a consultant to the National Endowment for the Humanities and has received the Mark Van Doren and Society of Columbia Graduates' Great Teachers Awards. He also serves as a consultant for CBS, NBC, and ABC educational programs.

COVER ILLUSTRATION
Gary McElhaney

MAPS
Go Media, Inc.

PHOTOGRAPHY CREDITS